The Woman of Genesis

Br. Thomas Mary Sennott, M.I.C.M.

Loreto Publications
Fitzwilliam, N.H. 03447
A.D. 2010

Copyright © 1984
by Thomas Mary Sennott

All Rights Reserved

Nihil obstat:
  Giles Dimock, O.P., S.T.D.

Imprimatur:
  +Bernard J. Flanagan
    Bishop of Worcester
  September 28, 1983

The *Nihil obstat* and *Imprimatur* are official declarations that a book or pamphlet is free of doctrinal or moral error. No implication is contained therein that those who have granted the *Nihil obstat* or *Imprimatur* agree with the contents, opinions or statements expressed.

ISBN: 0-911218-20-3 (Clothbound)
ISBN: 0-911218-19-X (Paperbound)

LIBRARY OF CONGRESS CATALOGING IN PUBLICATION DATA

Sennott, Thomas Mary.
  The Woman of Genesis.

  Bibliography: p.
  Includes Index.
   1. Bible. O.T. Genesis III, 15—Criticism, interpretation, etc.
   2. Mary, Blessed Virgin, Saint—Biblical teaching. 3. Typology
  (Theology)   I. Title.
  BS1235.2.S46 1984   222'.11064   84-9962

PRINTED IN THE UNITED STATES OF AMERICA

Published with permission by
Loreto Publications
P. O. Box 603   Fitzwilliam, NH 03447
Phone: 603-239-6671   www.LoretoPubs.org
ALL RIGHTS RESERVED - 2010

Printed and Bound in the USA
ISBN 978-1-930278-89-6

For
Our Lady
and
Saint Jerome

CONTENTS

Introduction	v
Acknowledgments	vii
The First Meeting The Historical Setting	1
The Second Meeting An Introduction to Biblical Criticism	21
The Third Meeting "He" versus "She"	37
The Fourth Meeting "Bruise" versus "Crush"	61
Works Cited	82

INTRODUCTION

In the book of Genesis we read that after our first parents fell, God promised them a future Redeemer. This passage, Genesis 3:15, is called the *Protoevangelium*, or "first good news." In the old Douay-Rheims Bible, which is a faithful translation of the Latin Vulgate of St Jerome, it reads:

> I will put enmities between thee and the woman,
>   and thy seed and her seed:
> she shall crush thy head,
>   and thou shalt lie in wait for her heel.

But in newer English translations, such as the Catholic edition of the Revised Standard Version, we find:

> I will put enmity between you and the woman,
>   and between your seed and her seed;
> he shall bruise your head
>   and you shall bruise his heel."

What is the reason for this change? Does this mean that the old version was wrong? To answer these questions I have imagined a dialogue between two fictional Catholics, Fr. Staatz who presents the case for the new reading, and Mrs. Stepan who defends the old. My own position is that of Mrs. Stepan, though I have tried to present Fr. Staatz's

The Woman of Genesis

case as fairly as possible. For the sake of simplicity and clarity, no attempt has been made to dramatize the dialogue, and each speaker presents his complete argument without interruption, a completely idealized situation, which unfortunately could probably never happen in the give and take of the real world.

St. Benedict Priory,
Still River, Massachusetts

ACKNOWLEDGMENTS

I would like to thank Fr. Richard Gilsdorf for his kind corrections, suggestions, and encouragement, and also Fr. Thomas Carleton for his wonderful enthusiasm and many valuable scriptural insights. But I would especially like to show my appreciation to Dom Rembert Sorg, O.S.B., who urged me to have Mrs. Stepan meet Fr. Staatz more on his own Scriptural grounds rather than relying solely on the authority of the Magisterium. Moreover, Dom Sorg provided me with several significant suggestions as to how this could be achieved. If I have failed to realize this convincingly, the fault lies only with me.

My deepest gratitude is also due to Fr. Giles Dimock, O.P. without whom this little book would never have seen the light of day, and to George Manuel Samano who generously helped with the production of the book just because it was about Our Lady.

Finally I would like to express my gratitude to the following publishers for the use of copyrighted material: to Creation-Life Publishers of San Diego, California for excerpts from *Ebla Tablets: Secrets of a Forgotten City* by Clifford Wilson, copyright © Master Books, Creation-Life Publishers, 1979; to Doubleday and Co. of Garden City, New York for excerpts from *Psalms (I)* (Anchor Bible) translated and edited by Fr. Mitchell Dahood, S.J., copyright © Anchor Books, Doubleday and Co., 1965, 1966; to the Liturgical Press of St. John's Abbey, Collegeville, Minnesota for

The Woman of Genesis

excerpts from *The Men and the Message of the Old Testament* by Fr. Peter Ellis, C.SS.R., copyright © The Liturgical Press, 1963; to Lumen Christi Press of Houston, Texas for excerpts from *A Companion to Scripture Studies* (Volume II) by Msgr. John Steinmueller, copyright © Lumen Christi Press, 1969; to Prow Books of the Franciscan Marytown Press, 1600 W. Park Avenue, Libertyville, Illinois for excerpts from the article *What is Guadalupe?* by Dr. Charles Wahlig and Fr. Bernard Geiger, O.F.M., Conv. in *A Handbook on Guadalupe*, copyright © Prow Books, Franciscan Marytown Press, 1974; and to Van Nostrand Reinhold (U.K.) of Wokingham, Berkshire, England for excerpts from the article *Genesis* by Fr. Bruce Vawter, C.M. in *A Catholic Commentary on Holy Scripture* edited by Fuller, Johnston and Kearns, copyright © Van Nostrand Reinhold, 1969.

The First Meeting

The Historical Setting

Scene: Aquinas Hall at Cheverus College, a large Catholic institution. The capacity audience is composed of students, faculty, and invited guests. Seated on the platform are the two parties in the dialogue, Fr. Robert A. Staatz and Mrs. Maria Stepan.

Fr. Robert A. Staatz

Good evening, and welcome to Cheverus College. For those of you who don't know me, my name is Robert Staatz, and I am the head of the Philosophy Department here at Cheverus. On the platform with me is Mrs. Maria Stepan of our History Department. For the past several weeks, Mrs. Stepan and I have conducted a private dialogue on the Woman of Genesis, the famous passage, Genesis 3:15, known as the *Protoevangelium*, or "first good news." Now, as many of you know, I am considered rather liberal or progressive, while Mrs. Stepan is considered very conservative or traditional; so, as you can imagine, our interpretations of the Woman of Genesis differ considerably. We thought the matter of sufficient interest and importance to continue the dialogue in public. The idea met with a great deal of enthusiasm, and we decided to arrange for four public meetings. Tonight's meeting is intended merely as an introduction and to give the historical setting of our Scriptural passage. For the sake of simplicity we have agreed always to keep the same format: namely, that I would present the so-called liberal position first, while Mrs. Stepan would present the conservative position second.

So without further comment, let me begin by reading out text from the Catholic edition of the Revised Standard Version, which I consider the best of the current English versions of the Bible.

> I will put enmity between you and the woman,
>   and between your seed and her seed;
> he shall bruise your head
>   and you shall bruise his heel.

The Pentateuch, the first five books of the Bible, was traditionally thought to have been the work of Moses, who was believed to have lived around 1500 B.C. But more recent biblical scholarship has established that the Pentateuch is the work of several unknown authors, whom Julius Wellhausen, a famous Protestant scholar who lived around the turn of the century, called the Yahwist, Elohist, Deutronomist, and Priestly Authors, or J E D P, for short. All of these authors are thought to have lived long after the time of Moses.

The entire first chapter of Genesis is called the Hexameron, or six days of creation, and was written by the so-called "Priestly Author" during the time of the Babylonian Captivity, around 600 to 500 B.C. This Priestly Author who preferred the name *Elohim* for God, continues through Chapter 2 to verse 4. Then right in the middle of the verse, Genesis 2:4b, we read:

> These are the generations of the heaven and

The First Meeting

the earth, when they were created, in the day that the *Lord God* made the earth and the heavens.

The phrase "Lord God" tells us that we are dealing with a different author, one whom Wellhausen called the "Yahwist Author." The phrase "Lord God" in Hebrew is *Adonai Elohim*, and the Hebrews substituted *Adonai*, Lord, out of reverence for the holy name Yahweh, "I am who am." The Yahwist or "J" author is now thought to have written around the time of Solomon, that is, around 900 B.C.

But before we can even begin to look at our text itself, we have to do what the Germans call a *Sitz im Leben*, that is, to put this passage in its proper historical setting; and only after that can we begin to examine its literal meaning. Let me quote now a popular introductory text on the study of the Bible, which is used in many Catholic colleges, including Cheverus. It is *The Men and the Message of the Old Testament*, by the Redemptorist Peter Ellis:

> The historical milieu of the Yahwist according to most authors is the reign of Solomon. It is the time consequently of Israel's greatest glory as a nation. It is a time also of danger to Israel's faith. Solomon, like Saul, is forgetting the place of monarchy in God's plan for Israel. The kingship of men is more important than the kingship of God. In the last decades of his reign, as a consequence of his marriages with Canaanite women and of his building Canaanite shrines even in Jerusalem, Solomon has not only given bad example to his people but has allowed Canaanite religion to threaten the true faith as it would a century later in the time of Achab and Jezabel.[1]

The Woman of Genesis

It is the general consensus among Scripture scholars today that the story of the Fall of our first parents is not an historical event. Rather, it is, among other things, a polemic against the fertility cults that were prevalent at the time of the Yahwist Author. Here is Peter Ellis's interpretation of our text:

> The meaning of the terms in the text, purposely vague so as not to destroy the elements of suspense for the audience, is quite clear to the mind of the author: the serpent is a symbol taken from the Canaanite fertility cults of the author's day and used to represent Satan, the archenemy of God and man, who is behind the nature worship of the Canaanites; the seed of the serpent represents the devotees of the fertility cults; the seed of the woman represents the Davidic dynasty through which God will bring to fulfillment His plan for the conquest of Satan and the salvation of the world; the woman who is associated with the dynasty in the work of conquest and salvation is the Queen-mother of the Davidic King.[2]

Adam and Eve are not now considered historical persons by contemporary biblical scholars because of the unanimous acceptance by the scientific community of the theory of the evolution of man. Let me turn now to Fr. Owen Garrigan, a professor of chemistry at Seton Hall University, and his excellent *Man's Intervention in Nature*, one of the volumes in the *Twentieth Century Encyclopedia of Catholicism*. Although most Catholic scholars accept the current scientific theory of the evolution of man, the problem of reconciling this theory with the Church's teaching

The First Meeting

on original sin has not yet been completely worked out. The term "polygenism" used by Garrigan is a Greek word meaning many pairs of first parents, while "monogenism" means one pair.

The new approach tries to separate as far as possible the biological question of polygenism from the theological question of original sin. In some respects this new understanding of Scripture is difficult to reconcile with traditional teaching. But, at least for the present, these tentative proposals seem to fit more harmoniously into a world view that takes evolution into account. (Polygenism seems to be biologically probable to provide a wide breeding base for the evolving human species. Moreover, the simultaneous occurrence of the critical "humanizing" mutation in both male and female individuals to produce the original pair seems improbable.)

Two lines of reinterpretation have issued from the vigorous biblical renaissance of our day:

1) Scripture scholars have suggested that "Adam" (literally, "the man") was used by the author of Genesis and other Old Testament writers to designate a corporate personality in the sense of the medieval "everyman." We can, indeed, see ourselves in the actions and reactions of Adam. The Adam encountered in the Hebrew Scriptures, therefore, was not a specific individual man in the intention of the sacred writers. It is also quite conceivable that St. Paul was not pronouncing on the question of the biological unity of

the human species when he spoke of the "second Adam." It seems, in fact, most probable that the question never occurred to him. Just as Christ's reference to the sign of Jonah does not guarantee the physical presence of Jonah in the belly of the whale, so Paul's reference to Christ as the second Adam does not guarantee physical monogenism.

2) Scriptural exegetes have recently given some prominence to the concept, quite general in biblical texts, of "sin of the world." The sacred authors were so keenly aware of the universality of sin and their own sinfulness that they formulated the story of everyman's fall. For them, the "sin of Adam" was a disordered will common to all those who share the human condition. It is the result of the free choice of man, but it is not restricted to one man's choice on a single occasion. In this view, the state of original sin in man depends on the condition of being human linking him to all mankind, rather than on the physical acts of generation linking him to a primal sinner.[3]

These ideas of Owen Garrigan are similar to those of Teilhard de Chardin, the famous scientist-theologian, whose opinions were the occasion of a *Monitum* or "Warning" issued by the Holy Office in 1962. But during Vatican II Teilhard was frequently quoted by many of the Council Fathers, and the "Pastoral Constitution on the Church in the Modern World" (*Gaudium et Spes*) owes much to his inspiration. On the occasion of the centenary of Teilhard's birth, Cardinal Casaroli, the Papal Secretary of State, sent a letter to Archbishop Poupard, the rector of the Catholic In-

The First Meeting

stitute of Paris and pro-president of Secretariat for Non-Believers. This letter read in part:

> The international scientific community and, more broadly, the whole intellectual world are preparing to celebrate the centenary of the birth of Fr. Teilhard de Chardin. The astonishing repercussions of his researches, together with the influence of his personality and the richness of his thought, have left a lasting mark on our age.
>
> The powerful insight into the value of nature, a keen perception of the dynamism of creation, a wide view of the becoming of the world were combined in him with undeniable religious fervour.
>
> Likewise due to his continual desire for dialogue with the science of his time and his dauntless optimism with regard to the evolution of the world, his intuitions, through the shimmer of words and the magic of images, caused a considerable stir.
>
> Geared to the future, this synthesis, often so lyrical in expression and fraught with a passion of the universal, will have contributed to restoring to man, tormented by doubt, the taste of hope.
>
> I am happy, your Excellency, to communicate this message to you on behalf of the Holy Father, for all the participants in the conference over which you preside at the Catholic Institute of Paris as a tribute to Fr. Teilhard de Chardin.[4]

So, in summary and conclusion, we have seen that our passage, Genesis 3:15, cannot be understood as an historical event. This new interpretation has been brought about by the advances in the science of biblical criticism, which we will discuss at our next meeting, but especially by the development of the theory of the evolution of man. As we know, there can be no real conflict between scientific truth and religious truth, which unfortunately was clearly the case with the older interpretation of this passage.

Mrs. Maria Stepan

Fr. Staatz began his presentation by reading our prophecy from the Revised Standard version of the Bible, which he prefers. Let me also begin tonight by reading this passage from the older Douay-Rheims version, which I prefer:

> I will put enmities between thee and the woman,
>   and thy seed and her seed:
> She shall crush thy head
>   and thou shalt lie in wait for her heel.

I would like to make a few comments on Fr. Staatz's contention that the Pentateuch was not written by Moses around 1500 B.C., as was traditionally believed, but by several unknown authors whom the liberal Protestant Julius Wellhausen called the Yahwist, Elohist, Deuteronomist, and Priestly Authors. Our text Genesis 3:15, he claims, was written by the Yahwist or "J" Author, who is supposed to have lived around 900 B.C., the time of Solomon. Now this contention does not stand up to a critical examination of the text. Let me turn to Msgr. John Steinmueller, a former consultor of the Pontifical Biblical Commission, who examines the internal evidence of the

The First Meeting

Pentateuch in some detail in his excellent *A Companion to Scripture Studies*. Msgr. Steinmueller lists six facts which emerge from an unbiased examination of the internal evidence:

1) The Pentateuch originated in the desert.
2) Residence outside Palestine is supposed.
3) An actual eyewitness is indicated.
4) The author is familiar with conditions in Egypt.
5) Canaan is unfamiliar to the writer.
6) Archaisms abound in the Pentateuch.

Let me just read Msgr. Steinmueller's presentation of his second point:

> *Residence outside Palestine Supposed.* There are certain factual details in the Pentateuch which presuppose the residence of the Hebrews outside Palestine. The wood employed by them for the construction of the Tabernacle is not cypress or cedar, but acacia or shittim, which is not found in Palestine but only in Egypt and the Sinaitic peninsula. The form of the Tabernacle resembles Egyptian temples, and the shape of the Ark of the Covenant is similar to the arks used by the Egyptians in their religious processions... The *tahash*...skins used in the construction of the Tabernacle seem to be from the gugong..., a herbivorous sea-animal resembling the manatee living in the Red Sea (Ex 25:5).[5]

Msgr. Steinmueller would be the first to admit, however, that internal evidence of this sort is of only secondary importance in determining the Mosaic authenticity of the Pentateuch. Of primary importance is the witness of history, or as Pope Leo XIII put it so well in his *Providentissimus Deus:*

> It is clear, on the other hand, that in historical questions, such as the origin and the handing down of writings, the witness of history is of primary importance, and that historical investigation should be made with the utmost care; and that in this matter internal evidence is seldom of great value, except as confirmation.[6]

In 1906, during the reign of Pope St. Pius X, the Pontifical Biblical Commission summarized the case for the Mosaic authorship of the Pentateuch in its condemnation of the Documentary Theory of Wellhausen:

> Whether the arguments amassed by critics to impugn the Mosaic authenticity of the sacred books designated by the name of Pentateuch are of sufficient weight notwithstanding the very many evidences to the contrary contained in both Testaments, taken collectively, the persistent agreement of the Jewish people the constant tradition of the Church, and internal arguments derived from the text itself, to justify the statement that these books have not Moses for their author but have been compiled from sources for the most part posterior to the time of Moses.
> *Answer:* In the negative.[7]

Let me go on now to Fr. Ellis's contention that the story

The First Meeting

of the Fall of our first parents is merely a polemical argument against the Canaanite fertility cults which involved the worship of serpents. Now, nowhere in the Bible is the serpent represented as a symbol of fertility, but rather as a symbol of the devil, a wise (in the sense of crafty) foe of God and man. The position of the serpent in the Bible is actually closer to the serpent in Egyptian mythology than it is to Canaanite mythology. In Egyptian mythology the serpent appears as a wise goddess, the minister of Amon-Ra, the sun-god. The Pharaoh wore on his forehead a royal ensign which was a carving of an asp (the Egyptian cobra) called the *uraeus*, presumably so he could partake of the wisdom and subtlety of that goddess. On the other hand, in Egyptian mythology, snakes, scorpions, worms, etc., were pictured as the fierce enemies of man in the after-life; and in particular the great serpent-god Apopis, the god of darkness, was thought to attack the barge of the sun-god Amon-Ra at sunrise and sunset. Since Moses was learned in all the wisdom of the Egyptians (Acts 7:22), it would seem more logical to maintain that Moses was influenced by the Egyptian view of the serpent rather than the Canaanite, but this would be another argument for the Mosaic authorship of the Pentateuch, which the liberals are unwilling to admit.

This does not mean, however, that the story of Adam and Eve is merely a purified form of some Egyptian serpent myth; indeed, it is much more likely that the Egyptian notion of the serpent is itself a corruption of a tradition handed down from the time of Adam which was preserved incorrupt only in the Bible. Let me read a few paragraphs from Pope Pius XII's encyclical *Humani Generis* which appeared in 1950:

The Woman of Genesis

Deplorable in particular is a certain fashion of interpreting too freely the historical books of the Old Testament. They wrongly quote in their favor a letter which the Pontifical Biblical Commission sent not long ago to the Archbishop of Paris. But this letter clearly points out that the first eleven chapters of Genesis, although they do not properly conform to the rules of historical composition used by the great Greek and Latin historians or by the historians of our time, do nevertheless pertain to history in a true sense to be further studied and determined by exegetes; that letter also says that the same chapters contain, in simple and metaphorical language adapted to the mentality of a people of low culture, the principle truths fundamental for our eternal salvation and a popular description of the origin of the human race and the chosen people. For the rest, if the ancient hagiographers have taken anything from popular narratives (and this may be conceded), we must not forget that they did so with the help of divine inspiration which preserved them from error in selecting and apprasing these documents.

In any case, whatever of popular narratives have found a place in the Sacred Scriptures must in no way be considered on a par with myths or other such things; these are more the product of an exuberant imagination than of that striving for truth and simplicity which is so apparent in the Sacred Books.[8]

Thus, there is no harm in saying that Moses, enlightened by divine inspiration, could have made use of some aspects of the Egyptian serpent lore with which he was familiar.

The First Meeting

We heard Msgr. Steinmueller suggest that Moses might have been influenced by Egyptian temples in his design of the Tabernacle, and that the Ark of the Covenant was similar to the arks used by the Egyptians in their religious processions, which Moses doubtless witnessed.

But there is no way we can establish the historicity of the story of Adam and Eve from the Bible alone, or even with the Bible aided by archaeology or any other science. That the story of Adam and Eve actually occurred in history has to be accepted on authority—the authority of the Church. Again in 1909 the Biblical Commission spelled out in detail just what we must take in the literal historical sense in the story of Adam and Eve:

> Whether, in particular, we may call in question the literal and historical meaning where there is question of facts narrated in these chapters which touch the fundamental teachings of the Christian religion; as for example: ...the special creation of man; the formation of the first woman from man; the unity of the human race; the original happiness of our first parents in a state of justice, integrity, and immortality; the divine command laid upon man to prove his obedience; the transgression of that divine command at the instigation of the devil under the form of a serpent; the fall of our first parents from their primitive state of innocence; and the promise of a future Redeemer.

Answer: In the negative.[9]

Let me go on now from Fr. Ellis to Fr. Owen Garrigan, and his contention that Adam, which means "the man," represents a corporate personality similar to the medieval notion of "everyman." If we look up "Adam" in a Hebrew lexicon such as Koehler-Baumgartner, we find:

אָדָם *adam* - a man, man, Adam.

There are no capital letters in Hebrew, so "adam" is ambiguous, and can mean either "a man," an indefinite individual, "man," a collective noun, or "Adam," a proper noun. Sometimes the definite article "the," which in Hebrew is a *he* ה pointed with a *patah* ַ , is prefixed to the noun to make it more determinate הָאָדָם "the man." For example in Genesis 1:26 we read: "Let us make *a* man (or simply "man")" אָדָם ; then in the following verse 27: "And God made *the* man הָאָדָם ." But proper nouns, "Adam," do not take the definite article, and we can only tell from the context that the first use of the proper noun in the Hebrew text is in Genesis 4:25: "*Adam* also knew his wife again." But it is so obvious that the collective noun "man" refers to a single man, that both the Greek Septuagint and the Latin Vulgate in violation of the Hebrew grammar (proper nouns do *not* take the definite article) render Genesis 2:19 and onward as "Adam." "And the Lord God having formed out of the ground all the beasts of the earth...brought them to *Adam* הָאָדָם to see what he would call them." So it is completely unscholarly to use the etymology of the word "Adam" as an argument for polygenism. Any honest reader will see that only a single individual is intended.

One of the best arguments from Scripture that Adam and Eve are a single pair (monogenism) and not a group (polygenism), is from Genesis 3:20. "And Adam called the name of his wife Eve: because she was the mother of *all the living*" (Douay-Rheims). Now, unfortunately, the translation "all the living" gives the impression that Eve is the mother of all the living animals as well as all the living men. Again if you look up the word for "living," which is *hay*, in a Hebrew lexicon (cf. Koehler-Baumgartner, 1967 ed.), its third meaning is: "kin, family, *all the descendants of the same mother and father.*" So a better translation of Genesis 3:20 would be: "And Adam called the name of his wife Eve: because she was the mother of *the whole family.*" That this is the meaning intended by Moses is demonstrated by the fact that, in the genealogies which follow Genesis 3:20, all the nations of the world trace their origin back to Adam and Eve. Therefore, there is no way from Scripture that you can argue that Adam and Eve represent a group (polygenism); the Scripture is perfectly clear that Adam and Eve are a single pair (monogenism).

Moreover, Fr. Garrigan's notion of original sin, the "sin of Adam," as "a disordered will common to all those who share the human condition," is certainly not Scriptural. A disordered will is one of the effects of original sin, not original sin itself.

Let me cite a few paragraphs from the article on original sin in the *Catholic Biblical Encyclopedia* by Msgr. John Steinmueller and Sr. Kathryn Sullivan, R.S.C.J.:

> Although Paul is the first inspired writer to explain clearly original sin, traces or allusions to it occur in the Old Testament. Mankind was always conscious of its sinful condition (1 Kgs 8:46; Job 4:17; 15:14; 25:4; Prov 20:9; Eccles 7:21; Sir 8:6), and this sinful state was even traced back to the sin of our first parents (Gen 2:17,25; 3:6f; Wis 2:24; Sir 25:33; Ps 50:7; cf. also 4 Esd 3:21; 4:30); but nowhere does the Old

Testament speak of the nature and guilt of original sin. Paul, however, explicitly stresses the nature and guilt of original sin in his Epistle to the Romans (5:12-21).[10]

The traditional Catholic teaching on original sin was reiterated in 1968 by Pope Paul VI in his *Creed of the People of God*. This creed was intended in part as a rebuttal to the many doctrinal errors expressed in the then recently published *Dutch Catechism*, among which was the Teilhardian notion of original sin as a disordered will common to the human condition:

> We believe that in Adam all have sinned, which means that the original offense committed by him caused human nature, common to all men, to fall to a state in which it bears the consequences of that offense, and which is not the state in which it was originally in our first parents, established as they were in holiness and justice, and in which man knew neither evil nor death. It is human nature so fallen, stripped of the grace that clothed it, injured in its own natural powers and subjected to the dominion of death, that is transmitted to all men, and it is in this sense that every man is born in sin. We therefore hold, with the Council of Trent, that original sin is transmitted with human nature, "not by imitation, but by propagation" and that it is thus "in each of us as his own."[11]

The main reason the liberals are forced to deny the historicity of the biblical account of the Fall, is, as Fr. Garrigan admitted, that they feel they have to accept the current scientific theory of the evolution of man. This theory demands a wide breeding base for a so-called "humanizing" mutation to have any possible chance of success, mathematically speaking. This would mean many Adams and Eves, or polygenism—as opposed to monogenism, one Adam and Eve, Now the defined doctrine of original sin depends on monogenism. We all sinned in Adam, and by baptism we become one with Christ. So, as Our Lord is one Person, Adam is one person, and as Our Lady is one person, Eve is one person. Let me quote one more paragraph from Pope Pius XII's encyclical *Humani Generis*:

> But as regards another conjecture, namely so-called polygenism, the children of the Church by no means enjoy the same liberty. No Catholic can hold that after Adam there existed on this earth true men who did not take their origin through natural generation from him as from the first parent of all, or that Adam is merely a symbol for a number of first parents. For it is unintelligible how such an opinion can be squared with what the sources of revealed truth and the documents of the Magisterium of the Church teach on original sin, which proceeds from sin actually committed by an individual Adam, and which, passed on to all by way of generation, is in everyone as his own.[12]

This condemnation of polygenism was repeated as recently as 1966 by Pope Paul VI:

> It is therefore evident that the explanations of

original sin given by some modern authors will seem to you irreconcilable with the true Catholic doctrine. Starting with the undemonstrated premise of polygenism, they deny, more or less clearly, that the sin from which so many cesspools of evil have come to mankind was first of all the disobedience of Adam, "first man," figure of that future Man, committed at the beginning of history.[13]

Let me now proceed from Fr. Garrigan to Fr. Teilhard de Chardin, whose teachings on Adam and Eve, polygenism, and original sin were the occasion of a *Monitum* or "Warning" issued by the Holy Office in 1962:

> Several works of Fr. Pierre Teilhard de Chardin, some of which were posthumously published, are being edited and are gaining a good deal of success.
> Prescinding from a judgment about those points that concern the positive sciences, it is sufficiently clear that the above mentioned works abound in such ambiguities, and indeed even serious errors, as to offend Catholic doctrine.
> For this reason, the most eminent and revered Fathers exhort all Ordinaries, as well as the superiors of Religious institutes, rectors of seminaries, and presidents of universities, effectively to protect the minds, particularly of youth, against the dangers presented by the works of Fr. Teilhard de Chardin and his followers.[14]

The letter of Cardinal Casaroli to Archbishop Poupard on the occasion of the celebration in honor of the cen-

The First Meeting

tenary of Teilhard's birth seems to have been the occasion of some confusion regarding the status of the *Monitum* concerning him issued in 1962. The situation was clarified, however, by a news release from the Vatican Press Office a few weeks later:

> Some organs of the press have interpreted the letter addressed by the Cardinal Secretary of State to His Excellency Archbishop Poupard on the occasion of the centenary of the birth of Fr. Teilhard de Chardin as a revision of the preceding position taken by the Holy See regarding this author, and in particular by the *Monitum* of the Holy Office dated June 30th, 1962, which pointed out that the author's work contains ambiguities and serious doctrinal errors.
>
> The question has been asked whether that interpretation has a basis.
>
> After consulting the Cardinal Secretary of State and the Cardinal Prefect of the Sacred Congregation of the Doctrine of the Faith, which, by disposition of the Holy Father, had been duly consulted regarding the letter in question, we are able to reply in the negative. Far from constituting a revision of the preceding position taken by the Holy See, the letter of Cardinal Casaroli expresses in various passages certain reservations—reservations which some newspapers passed over in silence—which referred precisely to the *Monitum* of June, 1962, even though this document is not precisely mentioned.[15]

Let me say, therefore, in summary and conclusion, that it is the testimony of the Bible itself, and the constant

The Woman of Genesis

teaching of the Tradition and Magisterium of the Church, that our passage—Genesis 3:15—was written by Moses himself, and is not a fictional polemic; but that it is, on the contrary, an actual historical account which must be understood in its obvious and literal sense.

REFERENCES

1. Peter Ellis, C.SS.R., *The Men and the Message of the Old Testament*, Liturgical Press, Collegeville, MN, 1963, p.324.
2. Ellis, *Op. cit.*, p.323
3. Owen Garrigan, *Man's Intervention in Nature*, Hawthorne Books, New York, 1967, pp.99,100.
4. *L'Osservatore Romano*, 22 June, 1981, p.2.
5. Msgr. John Steinmueller, *A Companion to Scripture Studies (Vol. 2)*, Lumen Christi Press, Houston, TX, 1969, p.21.
6. *Rome and the Study of Scripture*, Abbey Press, St. Meinrad, IN, 1964, p.52.
7. *Rome and the Study of Scripture*, p.43
8. Pope Pius XII, *Humani Generis*, 1950, Weston College Press, Weston, MA, 1951, p.45
9. *Idem*, p.56.
10. Msgr. John Steinmueller and Sr. Kathryn Sullivan, R.S.C.J., *Catholic Biblical Encyclopedia*, Joseph F. Wagner, Inc. New York, 1950, pp.595,596.
11. Msgr. Eugene Kevane, *Creed and Catechetics*, Christian Classics, Westminster, MD, 1978, p.8. cf. Denzinger 1513.
12. Pope Pius XII, *Op. cit.*, p.8.
13. Patrick O'Connell, *Original Sin in the Light of Present-Day Science*, Lumen Christi Press, Houston, TX, 1950, p.91.
14. Msgr. Leo Schumacher, *The Truth about Teilhard*, Twin Circle Publishing Co., New York, 1968, p.11.
15. *The Wanderer*, July 23, 1981. St. Paul, MN, pp.1,6.

THE SECOND MEETING

An Introduction to Biblical Criticism

Scene: Aquinas Hall, Cheverus College.

Fr. Robert A. Staatz

Good evening, and welcome again to Cheverus College. At our last meeting I read an interpretation of Genesis 3:15 by the Redemptorist Peter Ellis, in which he stated that our passage was written by the so-called Yahwist Author about the time of Solomon, and was intended as a polemic against the Canaanite fertility cults. This interpretation is based on a relatively new science called "biblical criticism," which began in Germany around the middle of the nineteenth century.

The science of biblical criticism can be divided into two main branches, the first of which was originally known by the awkward name of "higher criticism," which fortunately has been replaced by the more felicitous phrase "literary criticism." This literary criticism can, in turn, be subdivided into three parts. In the first part, called "source criticism," the critic tries to recover both the author and the historical setting of a particular text. This was the technique Ellis used to determine that our text was written by the Yahwist Author around the time of Solomon. In the second part, called "form criticism," Ellis determined that the literary

The Woman of Genesis

form of our passage was that of a polemic against the Canaanite fertility cults. This meant that our account was not an historical event, but rather fictional, though of course written for a religious purpose. Finally, in the third part called "redaction criticism," we find that our passage must have been reworked by a redactor or editor into the final form we have today. The original Yahwist Author would not have had any notion of a personal Messiah, which was a late development in the religious history of the Jews. This Redactor is generally thought to be someone like the scribe Ezra, who lived around 400 B.C., the time of the Restoration.

Now I realize that, at first glance, it might seem arbitrary to date the Yahwist Author around 900 B.C., and the Redactor in the fourth century B.C., but this is also done scientifically. The dating was originally determined by a German scientific school called the *Religionsgeschichte*, which means the study of "the history (or evolution) of religions." This field of study is presently the province of the sciences of cultural anthropology and ethnology. Since it is now universally accepted that we have developed from lower animals, the first men could only have had a primitive language and a crude notion of religion. Scientists have not yet worked out a completely satisfactory theory of the evolution of religion, but one of the many versions available holds that the first men were animists, that is, that they merely worshipped the forces of nature. A later stage of development, polytheism, personalized those various forces. A still further development is called henotheism, in which a particular tribal god was considered superior to neighboring tribal gods. Some members of this school thought that Moses was a henotheist, and thus incapable of

The Second Meeting

writing the Pentateuch as we now have it. Finally monotheism, or the worship of one supreme God, did not develop until the time of the prophets, especially the so-called "Second Isaiah," who wrote around 600 B.C., the time of the Babylonian Captivity.

So much for literary criticism and its scientific base. The other main branch of biblical criticism was once called "lower criticism," but now, happily, "textual criticism." Textual criticism as a scientific discipline seeks to recover the original text of the Bible, because it is only in the original text that the Bible was actually inspired. In the case of Genesis 3:15, this means that we must try to recover the original Hebrew text of the Yahwist Author, who wrote about 900 B.C. We, of course, have no Hebrew text from that early date. Our oldest Hebrew manuscripts go back only to the early Middle Ages. So we have to try to recover the original text by a comparison with various Greek and Latin translations, the manuscripts of which go back almost to the time of Christ. This is, of course, no easy task, and is the reason there are always new and better versions of the Bible being brought out.

Let me now give a brief review of some of the many English versions of the Bible. In 1609, during the English persecution, a group of Catholic biblical scholars fled to Douay in what is now Belgium, and produced the famous Douay-Rheims version. This version, as we have seen, renders our passage thus:

> I will put enmities between thee and the woman,
>   and between thy seed and her seed:
> *She* shall crush thy head,
>   and thou shalt lie in wait for *her* heel.

The Woman of Genesis

A few years later, in 1611, Protestant scholars produced the King James version, a big improvement, we will see, over the Douay. It reads:

> I will put enmity between thee and the woman,
>   and thy seed and her seed:
> *It* shall bruise thy head
>   and thou shall bruise *his* heel.

In 1962 the Confraternity of Christian Doctrine came a little closer to the better Protestant version. In more modernized English it reads:

> I will put enmity between you and the woman,
>   and your seed and her seed:
> *He* shall crush your head
>   and you shall lie in wait for *his* heel.

Finally in 1970 came the Revised Standard Version, a revision of the original King James version. In the so-called "Catholic edition," the seven books of the Old Testament considered aprocryphal by Protestants but deuterocanonical by Catholics, have been added; otherwise the text is substantially the same in both Protestant and Catholic editions. It is considered the best to date of the new ecumenical Bibles. Here again is its version of Genesis 3:15:

> I will put enmity between you and the woman
>   between your seed and her seed;
> *He* shall bruise your head
>   and you shall bruise *his* heel.

The Second Meeting

Let me conclude this cursory introduction to biblical criticism by reading a few passages from Pope Pius XII's marvelous encyclical *Divino Afflante Spiritu*, which ended the long Modernist "witch hunt," and launched the still-flourising renaissance in Catholic biblical studies. The Holy Father is here speaking of textual criticism:

> The great importance which should be attached to this kind of criticism was aptly pointed out by Augustine when, among the precepts to be recommended to the student of the Sacred Books, he put in the first place the care to possess a corrected text. "The correction of the codices"—so says this most distinguished Doctor of the Church—"should first of all engage the attention of those who wish to know the divine Scripture so that the uncorrected may give place to the corrected." In the present day this art, called textual criticism, is used with great and praiseworthy results in the editions of profane writings, and is also rightly employed in the case of the Sacred Books because of that very reverence which is due to the Divine Oracles. For its very purpose is to insure that the sacred text be restored as perfectly as possible, purified from the corruptions due to the carlessness of the copyists, and be freed, as far as may be done, from glosses and omissions which are wont to make their way gradually into writings handed down through many centuries.
>
> It is scarcely necessary to observe that this criticism, which some fifty years ago not a few made use of quite arbitrarily and often in such wise that one would say they did so to introduce into the sacred text their

own preconceived ideas, has rules so firmly established and secure today that it has become a most valuable aid to the purer and more accurate editing of the sacred text, and any abuse can easily be discovered. Nor is it necessary here to call to mind—since it is doubtless familiar and evident to all students of Sacred Scripture—to what extent the Church has held in honor these studies in textual criticism from the earliest centuries down even to the present day.

Today, therefore, since this branch of science has attained to such a high perfection, it is the honorable, though not always easy, task of students of the Bible to procure by every means that, as soon as possible, editions of the Sacred Books and of ancient editions may be duly published by Catholics in accordance with those standards which unite the greatest reverence for the sacred text with an exact observance of all the rules of criticism. And let all know that this prolonged labor is not only necessary for the right understanding of the divinely-given writings, but also is urgently demanded by that piety through which it behooves us to be grateful to the God of all providence, Who from the throne of His majesty has sent these books as so many paternal letters to his own children.[1]

So in conclusion, let me say again that a biblical text is inspired only in the language in which it was originally written. Our passage was written in Hebrew, and unfortunately our oldest Hebrew texts go back only to the early Middle Ages. This means that to recover the original text we will have to compare it with older Greek and Latin translations which go back almost to the time of Christ. This is the special province of that branch of biblical criticism called textual criticism, and we will see it in action at our next meeting when we discuss the relative merits of the "He" versus "She" wordings of our various texts.

Mrs. Maria Stepan

All forms of biblical criticism are legitimate aids to the study of the Bible if they are used in a proper manner, that is in a manner which harmonizes with the Tradition and Magisterium of the Church. Fr. Peter Ellis's use of source criticism, the Documentary Theory of Julius Wellhausen, is contrary to the constant Tradition of the Church and in defiance of the condemnation of that theory by the Magisterium. But let me give an example of a legitimate use of source criticism. We saw that, in 1906, the Biblical Commission condemned the Documentary or Four-Source Theory, and upheld the Mosaic authenticity of the Pentateuch; but at the same time it stated that Moses himself undoubtedly used sources in his writings:

> Whether it may be granted, without prejudice to the Mosaic authenticity of the Pentateuch, that Moses employed sources in the production of his work, i.e., written documents or oral traditions, from which, to suit his special purpose and under the influence of divine inspiration, he selected some things and inserted them into his work, either literally or in substance, summarized or amplified.
>
> Answer: In the affirmative.[2]

The Woman of Genesis

Here is an example of a traditional use of source criticism, and since it is in harmony with the Tradition and Magisterium of the Church, it makes more sense Scripturally. This is again from Msgr. Steinmueller:

Moses as Redactor. The scholars of the traditional school commonly admit that Moses made use of oral and written sources in writing the Pentateuch. For the Book of Genesis he employed various ancient traditions, which for the most part were oral and were faithfully preserved and transmitted among the individual tribes. This may at times explain the variations in vocabulary and in the divine names, and Moses may have occasionally even conflated separate traditions about one and the same fact. It is also possible that Moses employed documents for the legislative sections of his work. In the ethical, civil, and criminal legislation he made use of juristic terminology and formularies which were similar to other Semitic legal codes, but in the priestly and ceremonial laws (which critics call P), which are proper to the Hebrews, Moses appears as the legislator. Thus, the peculiarities of language and style, which critics ascribe to various collectors or redactors, are to be attributed to Moses himself, who made use of his sources in varying manners.[3]

Let me now proceed from source criticism to form criticism, or the study of the various literary forms of the Bible. At our last meeting, we heard Fr. Peter Ellis claim that the literary form of Genesis 3:15 was not history, as had been traditionally believed, but rather a fictional

The Second Meeting

polemic against the Canaanite fertility cults. The liberals also claim that the literary form of the first chapter of Genesis, which deals with the creation of the world, is a purified form of a pagan myth. Now, these claims are based on what the Germans call the *Religionsgeschichte*, the study of the history or evolution of religions. According to this theory, Moses would have been incapable of writing the story of creation because the notion that the world was created by God out of nothing was a much later development in the history of religion. Now the great appeal of biblical criticism, including form criticism, is that it is supposed to be "scientific, " but many of these literary theories are in conflict with another science, that of biblical archaeology.

The most recent significant findings in biblical archaeology have been at Ebla, in Syria, where thousands of clay tablets covered with cuneiform writing have been discovered. These tablets have been dated at around 2400 B.C., or about a thousand years before the time of Moses. Let me read a few excerpts from *Elba Tablets: Secrets of a Forgotten City*, by Dr. Clifford Wilson, a Protestant biblical archaeologist. Remember that the *Religionsgeschichte* claims Moses could not have written that God created the world out of nothing, because the doctrine of creation did not develop until around 600 B.C., the time of the "Priestly Author," whom they claim as the author of the Hexameron:

A New Creation Tablet

He [Professor Pettinato, the epigrapher working on the tablets] said that the record appeared to be

The Woman of Genesis

remarkably like that found in the first verses of Genesis."In the beginning God created the heavens and the earth"...he said that the creation tablet was closer to Genesis chapter 1 than anything yet discovered. It said that there was a time when there was no heaven, and Lugal ("the great one") formed it out of nothing; there was no earth, and Lugal made it; there was no light, and he made it.[4]

Moreover, the *Religionsgeschichte* maintains that Moses would not have been capable of writing a law code around 1500 B.C., because the high ethical monotheism of the Mosaic Code did not evolve until around the time of the so-called "Second Isaiah," who is also supposed to have lived around 600 B.C., the time of the Babylonian Captivity. Here again is Dr. Wilson speaking of the law code that existed at Ebla around 2400 B.C., one thousand years before the time of Moses:

> Two tablets deal with case law, and the law code of Ebla must now be recognized as the oldest ever yet found. In dealing with the penalties for injuries, distinction is made according to the nature of the act. An injury caused by a blow of the hand merited a different penalty from one caused by a weapon such as a dagger. Different penalties are prescribed for various offenses.
> There is elaborate discussion of case law, with varying conditions recognized for what at first look might seem to be the same crime. In the case of a complaint involving sexual relations, if the girl was able to prove that she was a virgin and that the act was forced on

her, the penalty against the man was death. Otherwise he would pay a fine that varied according to the circumstances...

The Ebla laws dealing with sex offenses are remarkably close to those found in Deuteronomy 22:22-30. In that passage there is a distinction made according to whether the girl was a virgin and cried for help, or was a willing participant in the act. This is very close to the law at Ebla.[5]

One of the favorite statements of Protestant fundamentalists is that "archaeology proves the Bible." But of course we really don't need archaeology to know that the Bible is true; we have the authority of the Church. Neverthless, I find it fascinating that biblical archaeology always supports the Magisterium. We saw at our last meeting that in 1906 the Biblical Commission condemned the Documentary Theory of Wellhausen; in 1909 it also condemned the idea that the first chapter of Genesis was a purified form of a pagan myth. These decisions are clearly supported by the findings at Ebla.

Let me conclude my discussion of the *Religionsgeschichte* with Msgr. Steinmueller's comments:

> This rationalistic interpretation and evolutionary conception of Hebrew history cannot be accepted. It precludes the possibility of any revealed religion, miracles, and prophecies. It also denies the objective reality and setting of Old Testament books, and bases their interpretation largely upon subjectivism. We know that true monotheism existed among the Hebrews from the very beginning under Abraham,

the father of the Hebrew race (cf. Gen 18:25;24:3 supposedly in J) and that the prophets in the most emphatic manner preach absolute monotheism and condemn idolatry as a violation of the Mosaic Sinaitic Covenant.

The basic thesis of the critics that, in the science of religion, monotheism is the ultimate result and culmination of progressive evolution among peoples, cannot be sustained. The learned anthropologist, Rev. W. Schmidt, S.V.D., has proved conclusively that the outstanding mark of the religion of primitive people is its fundamental monotheism (i.e., their belief in one Supreme Being). Professor Langdon has defended the thesis that the early Sumerians were originally monotheists and Lagrange did the same for the early Semites.

The internationally known biblical scholar, Professor Johann Goetsburger of Munich, is thus correct when he writes: "The prevailing Pentateuchal theories in particular instances are still unconsciously derived from or consciously influenced by preconceived notions of religious or historic evolution, which by no means can be regarded as permanent scientific conclusions.[6]

Let me now move on from form criticism to textual criticism, by means of which the scholar tries to recover the text in which the Sacred Book was originally written. Pope St. Pius X required all priests, especially teachers in seminaries and Catholic universities, to take an oath against Modernism, which especially singled out the abuse of this otherwise legitimate tool of biblical studies:

The Second Meeting

Furthermore, with due reverence, I submit and adhere with my whole heart to the condemnation, declarations, and all the prescripts contained in the encyclical *Pascendi* and in the decree *Lamentabili*, especially those concerning what is known as the history of dogmas. [This is again a reference to the *Religionsgeschichte*.]

I also reject the error of those who say that the faith held by the Church can contradict history, and that the Catholic dogmas, in the sense in which they are now understood, are irreconcilable with a more realistic view of the origins of the Christian religion. I also condemn and reject the opinion of those who say that a well-educated Christian assumes a dual personality—that of a believer and at the same time of a historian; as though it were permissible for a historian to hold things that contradict the faith of the believer, or to establish premises which, provided there be no direct denial of dogmas, would lead to the conclusion that dogmas are either false or doubtful. Likewise, I reject the method of judging and interpreting Sacred Scripture which, departing from the Tradition of the Church, the analogy of faith, and the norms of the Apostolic See, embraces the misrepresentations of the rationalists and with no prudence or restraint adopts textual criticism as the one and supreme norm.[7]

The reason Pope St. Pius singled out textual criticism especially, is that in the hands of the Modernists it had become merely a variation of the Protestant principle of *sola Scriptura*, Scripture alone, or private interpretation of the

Bible. Let me conclude by reading from an excellent report on the current state of biblical studies by the Cardinal Archbishop of Osaka, Paul Taguchi, which appeared in *L'Osservatore Romano* in 1975:

> Of the many doctrinal deviations now being adopted by some so-called Catholic exegetes, perhaps the most harmful is the Protestant principle of *sola Scriptura*, or "Scripture alone." Those who uphold this principle assert that the only source of revelation is the Bible itself and completely ignore Tradition and the Magisterium of the Church. But this assertion is incompatible with the unity of Holy Scripture. It is as though they were trying to wrench the Holy Spirit who wrote the books from the same Holy Spirit who interprets them through the organs of Tradition. The falsity of this stand shows itself in two main tendencies.[8]

The two main tendencies are: first, "exegetical research is considered to be beyond the pale of the authority of the Magisterium," and second, "the opinions of contemporary exegetes, and particularly those of Protestants, are rated higher than those of the Fathers of the Church, and of Tradition." Let me just read Cardinal Taguchi's analysis of the first tendency:

> One comes across frequent references to a so-called "scientific investigation" of Sacred Scripture, as being in opposition to a "Catholic interpretation," almost as though the Magisterium and Tradition of the Church were superfluous to a correct understanding of the

The Second Meeting

Bible. Similarly the term "scientific or theological Magisterium" appears as the rival of the "Magisterium of the Church's authority." Consequently, total reliance is placed on the critical and historical methods of study, while Catholic interpretations are regarded as mere impositions.

This approach, in practice if not in theory, denies the Magisterium its right to guard, interpret, and explain Sacred Scripture. The important word here is *interpret*, for it is the Magisterium's supreme task to do this with the truths of faith in its care. The exegete, then, should do his work with the Magisterium as his support, directed by it, defended by it, joyfully submitting to it, in the sure knowledge that it is the Magisterium which maintains and has always maintained the continuity of the Church's teaching.

The last point is worth emphasizing, especially in reference to the interpretation criteria, for the Magisterium always proceeds in strict continuity. It would therefore be going against its very essence for the Magisterium to look on one of its documents in isolation from all the others that came before, as though it presented a brand new principle ignoring or disregarding the way things had always been understood previously. The only theological meaning possible for any given text of the Magisterium is one that links up with all that the Magisterium has declared previously, with Tradition, and with the analogy of faith.[9]

So let me conclude by saying again: we cannot find the meaning of a particular passage in the Bible by biblical criticism alone. This idea is but an extension of the Protestant principle of *sola Scriptura*, or private interpretation of the Bible. Legitimate biblical criticism, including textual criticism, is only an aid and can never be a substitute for the Tradition and Magisterium of the Church, which has been given us by God to reach an authentic interpretation of His Word.

REFERENCES

1. Pius XII, *Divino Afflante Spiritu*, (1943), reprinted in *Rome and the Study of Scripture*, Abbey Press, St. Meinrad, IN, 1964, pp.90,91.
2. *Rome and the Study of Scripture*, p.119.
3. Msgr. John Steinmueller, *A Companion to Scripture Studies* Vol. 2, Lumen Christi Press, Houston, TX, 1969, pp.67,68.
4. Clifford Wilson, *Elba Tablets: Secrets of a Forgotten City*, Master Books, Creation-Life Publishers, San Diego, CA, 1979, p.48.
5. Wilson, *Op. cit.*, pp.28,29.
6. Steinmueller, *Op. cit.*, pp.288,289.
7. The Jesuit Fathers of St. Mary's College, *The Church Teaches*, B. Herder Book Co., St. Louis, MO, 1955, pp.37,38; cf. Denzinger 2146.
8. Cardinal Paul Taguchi, *The Study of Sacred Scripture*, L'Osservatore Romano, May 15, 1975, pp.4,5.
9. Taguchi, *Op. cit.* p.5.

THE THIRD MEETING

"He" versus "She"

Scene: Aquinas Hall.

Fr. Robert A. Staatz

Good evening, and welcome once again to Cheverus College. Let me begin our third meeting by reading our two conflicting versions of Genesis 3:15. This is the Revised Standard Version which I prefer:

> I will put enmity between you and the woman.
>   and between your seed and her seed;
> He shall bruise your head
>   and you shall bruise his heel.

And here once more is the older Douay-Rheims version preferred by Mrs. Stepan:

> I will put enmities between thee and the woman,
>   and thy seed and her seed:
> She shall crush thy head,
>   and thou shalt lie in wait for her heel.

Now, you can see that the primary differences between the two versions are found in the second *distich* or couplet.

The Woman of Genesis

The "she" of the Douay has been changed to "he" in the Revised Standard; and "crush" to "bruise"; and "lie in wait for" again to "bruise." Tonight we would just like to examine the "he" versus "she," and in our final meeting we will consider "bruise" versus "crush."

Let me now turn to the Vincentian Bruce Vawter, the author of *A Path Through Genesis,* a book considered a classic in its field. Fr. Vawter is one of the world's leading authorities on the Book of Genesis, and he is the author of the article on Genesis in *A New Catholic Commentary on Holy Scripture.* Here are a few thoughts from this excellent article:

> Genesis 3:15 has traditionally been called the *Protoevangelium,* that is, the first proclamation of the good news of salvation. In this text there is that which is certain and that which continues to baffle the interpreter. Firstly, it is certain that the "enmity" of which the text speaks does not refer simply to the natural repugnance of woman for the serpent. "*I will put*" determines the enmity as one in which God plays a part. The enmity, then, is a moral one divinely willed between the woman and what the serpent represents. The "woman" in the context can only be the woman who appears throughout and who is addressed in the following verse, Eve, "the mother of all the living" (3:20). The "seed" of the woman is collective, referring to her descendants in general (as the "seed" of Abraham in 13:15; 17:7, etc.), therefore the entire human race. This is evident, since the "seed" of the serpent is also collective, that is, the powers of evil who will continue the work of the tempter throughout the history of the human race.[1]

The Third Meeting

Thus, to begin with, Bruce Vawter does not consider this passage a prophecy in the strict sense. The "she" of the Douay-Rheims has been used to give a Mariological interpretation to this passage, and the "he" of the Revised Standard to give a Messianic interpretation. But the Yahwist Author would not have had any notion of a personal Messiah, which, was a late development in Jewish history, and so by the "woman" of the passage, he could only have intended Eve. Bruce Vawter continues:

> "It," since the "seed" is collective, should be the translation of the Hebrew pronoun *hu*.[2]

Now, Vawter rejects the "she" of the Douay, and is actually not too happy with the "he" of the Revised Standard. Hebrew has no neuter pronoun, and "he" can also mean "it." So the *hu* would be better translated "it," since the pronoun is referring to "seed," a neuter noun. Collective nouns are usually neuter; you wouldn't use the pronoun "he," to refer to the collective noun "crowd," for instance, but rather "it." He goes on:

> The Greek Septuagint has *autos* ["he"] instead of the expected *auto* ["it"].[3]

This is textual criticism in action. Since the Hebrew is ambiguous, our critic turns to the Greek translation of the Old Testament known as the Septuagint, which dates from around 250 to 150 B.C. But here we find *autos*, the Greek word for "he," rather than the expected *auto* ("it").

> This is not necessarily due to dittography (*autos sou teresei*) ["he shall bruise your"] . . .[4]

43

The Woman of Genesis

(Fr. Staatz writes on the blackboard.)

αὐτός σου τηρήσει
auto(s) sou teresei
"he shall watch for your"

Dittography is a copyist's error. The final *sigma* (s) of *autos* αὐτός, "he," is followed by the *sigma* of *sou* σου, "your," so the copyist could have accidentally added an extra *sigma* to the *auto*, making the word "he" rather than "it."

...nor is this due to a slavish rendering of *hu* ["he"] (which is masculine to agree with the masculine *zera*, "seed"); nor does it testify to a personal Messianic interpretation on the part of the Septuagint. The identical...construction appears in the Septuagint of 2 Sm 7:12; 1 Chr 17:11, where as in Gen 3:15 the word *sperma* ["seed"], though neuter, is followed by a masculine pronoun: the translator could not forget that a human "seed" was in question whether collective or individual, and he therefore thought of *anthropos* "man," or *huios* "son," as the antecedent of the pronoun.[5]

So although Vawter would prefer "it," because the pronoun refers to the neuter "seed," he is explaining how it has happened to be rendered "he," since it is a human seed. He then proceeds to explain how this passage gradually acquired a Messianic interpretation, an interpretation which was certainly not in the mind of the original Yahwist Author, and probably not even of the late Redactor who reworked this passage.

The Third Meeting

There is no recognizable allusion to Gen 3:15 elsewhere in the Hebrew Bible, and it is not interpreted Messianically by either pre- or post-Christian Jewish exegesis. It is unlikely that there is any reference to it in Gal 4:4, Rom 16:20, or even Apoc 12. Irenaeus, following Justin, appears to have been the first to see in the text a personally Messianic reference to Christ; but more than half the Fathers, including the greatest Doctors of the East (Basil, Gregory Nazianzen, Chrysostom) and the West (Ambrose, Augustine, Jerome, Gregory), did not take it as Messianic at all. This, of course, does not mean that it is illegitimate for us today to employ sound exegetical principles to discern such a Messianic sense in the light of New Testament revelation and the development of Christian doctrine, as has been done by Coppens, Rigaux, and others.[6]

Bruce Vawter then comments on the later development of the Mariological interpretation of this passage:

The Mariological sense of the passage followed once it was recognized to have a personally Messianic application. The Vulgate [Latin translation of St. Jerome] reading, however, does not seem to be early Christian testimony to a Mariological interpretation.
The *ipsa* ["she"] reading is found in most of the Vulgate manuscripts, and even the relatively few that have *ipse* ["he"] have been "corrected" to *ipsa* by a subsequent hand; but in view of St. Jerome's statement cited above, it is doubtful that he translated *ipsa*.[7]

The Woman of Genesis

The statement which Vawter had cited earlier was:

> However, in his *Liber Hebraicarum questionum in Genesim* [*The Book of Hebrew Questions in Genesis*], he [Jerome] observes, having noted the *Vetus Latinus* [*Old Latin*] translation: "The Hebrew has it better: 'He will bruise your head.'"[8]

So Jerome himself preferred the "he" of the Hebrew. Vawter evidently thinks that the present *ipsa* reading of the Vulgate crept into the text by way of errors on the part of copyists.

> This reading is known to him [Jerome] and to Augustine, however. It appears to have come from Ambrose who was in this dependent on Philo Judaeus. Philo, arguing from a supposed rigid law of parallelism, maintained that the pronoun should pair with "woman" rather than with "seed," since the opposition in this member of the verb returned to that of the woman and the serpent. Neither Philo nor Ambrose interpreted 3:15 Messianically; to both of them "she" was the woman of the context, Eve.[9]

Philo is a Jewish philosopher who died around 40 A.D., and the parallelism to which he refers is a technique of Hebrew poetry in which one idea parellels another similar idea. Philo is saying that since the first *distich* or couplet refers to a woman, "I will put enmity between you and the woman," the second *distich* would have to parallel woman, and therefore should be rendered "she" rather than "he." But Vawter maintains that the parellelism of Hebrew

The Third Meeting

poetry is not intended to be that rigid, and that this interpretation does not square with the other evidence we have from biblical criticism. He concludes his comments with the development of the Mariological interpretation of this passage:

> The bulls *Ineffabilis Deus* (Dec 8, 1854) of Pius IX and *Munificentissimus Deus* (Nov 1, 1950) of Pius XII respectively defining the dogmas of the Immaculate Conception and the Assumption of Our Lady made use of the Messianic and Mariological interpretation of Gen 3:15 that later developed in Christian tradition.[10]

So in summary we see that, since the pronoun which is the subject of the phrase "shall bruise your head" refers to the "seed" of the preceding line, the pronoun should be rendered "it" to agree with "seed," a neuter noun. To use "she" as the subject makes no sense textually speaking, since both the Hebrew and Greek have "he." The *ipsa* of the Latin Vulgate most probably arose due to the errors of copyists, since St. Jerome himself, in his *Book of Hebrew Questions in Genesis*, states his preference for "he." The majority of the Fathers of the Church did not consider this passage Messianic, and its Mariological interpretation is an even later development.

Mrs. Maria Stepan

If we examine the various versions of the Bible that have appeared throughout the history of the Church, we find that the subject of the phrase, "shall crush thy head," has been rendered in three different ways, namely: "he," "she,"

The Woman of Genesis

and "it." Let me read a few excerpts from Cornelius a Lapide, the great Jesuit biblical scholar whose famous *Commentary on Sacred Scripture* appeared in 1544:

> The reading here is three-fold. The first is that of the Hebrew codices which have "It (that is, the seed) shall crush thy head," and so reads St. Leo and after him Lipomanus. The second is "He (namely, the man or Christ) shall crush thy head." So the Septuagint and Chaldaic. The third is "She shall crush thy head." So the Roman Bible and almost all the Latins read with St. Augustine, John Chrysostom [in Latin translation], Ambrose, Gregory, Bede, Alcuin, Bernard, Eucherius, Rupert, and others.[11]

The amazing thing is—and this is the continuous miracle of the Bible—that the theological meaning remains the same no matter which pronoun is used. Lapide continues:

> It should be noted that none of these readings should be rejected; on the contrary all are true. For when God, as here, forms an enmity between the woman and her seed, and the serpent and its seed, he means to indicate in what follows, that the woman with her seed is about to crush the serpent's head; and also on the other hand, that the serpent persecutes both the woman's heel and her seed's heel...
>
> These things apply...in the literal sense to Christ and to the Blessed Virgin as they fight against the devil. For the woman is Eve who crushed the devil when she did penance, or better, Mary, daughter of Eve; her seed is Jesus, and the Christian people; the

serpent is the devil, and his seed the infidels and all impious people. Therefore the Blessed Virgin Mary crushed the serpent, because she always fully and gloriously conquered the devil and all the heresies (which are the serpent's head), throughout the whole world, as the Church sings; Christ indeed, has most perfectly crushed his head and machinations, (the devil and all his kingdom,) and taken away his spoils, by His own power through the Cross; and as Christ, so penitent Eve, innocent Mary, and all of us received the power to crush the devil and his seed, (that is, his suggestions, and also impious men, for their father and prince is the devil). This is what is said in Psalm 90:12, "Thou shalt walk upon the asp and the basilisk: and thou shalt trample under foot the lion and the dragon." And Luke 10:19, "Behold I have given you power to tread upon serpents and scorpions, and upon all the power of the enemy: and nothing shall hurt you." And to Romans 16:20, "And the God of peace crush Satan under your feet speedily."[12]

You will remember that Fr. Vawter claimed there was no reference to Genesis 3:15 anywhere in the Bible. Therefore, granted that there is no difference theologically whether we use "he," "she," or "it," the question still remains: what did Moses actually write, or rather, as we shall see, how did he pronounce our pronoun?

So let us examine the Hebrew, Greek, and Latin readings of this passage in that order. In the original Hebrew written language, there were no vowels, only consonants. This means that one had to have an oral tradition to know how the written words were pronounced.

This, incidentally, is an excellent argument against the Protestant principle of *sola Scriptura*, "Scripture alone," or private interpretation of the Bible, which liberal Catholics have adopted. Fr. Staatz holds that the Bible was inspired only in the language in which it was originally written; and, while this is certainly true, it does not mean that the inspired written text substantiates itself, as *sola Scriptura* implies. There are two sources of revelation: Scripture and Tradition, and the two are interdependent. In the particular case of Genesis 3:15, we could not even read the passage at all without an explicit oral tradition; therefore, revelation as such had to extend both to the written word of God, Scripture, and the unwritten word of God, Tradition. Yet, even when we are enabled to read the written word properly, we still do not know what it means, especially in a difficult passage like the one under discussion. "Thinkest thou that thou understandest what thou readest?...How can I, unless some man show me?" (Acts 8:30,31). We need Tradition, the teachings of the Fathers, and the Magisterium of the Church, to understand what the Bible truly means. Thus, I hope to demonstrate that Genesis 3:15 provides us with a perfect test case confirming the Catholic doctrine of Scripture and Tradition, and rejecting the Protestant principle of *sola Scriptura*, as a means of reaching a proper interpretation of Holy Scripture.

The Massoretes, a group of Jewish scholars who lived between 800 and 900 A.D., tried to fix the oral tradition of Hebrew by inventing an arbitrary system of vowels now called "Massoretic points," or simply "points." Now, to be able to understand the "he" versus "she" problem, we should take a brief glance at the Hebrew language. At the

The Third Meeting

very minimum we need to have some idea of how the Massoretic points work.

(As Mrs. Stepan continues speaking, she writes on the blackboard.)

הוא

In the original text, our pronoun was written like this. Reading backwards, as we do in Hebrew, we have only the consonants *he* ה (pronounced HAY), *waw* ו , and *aleph* א. Thus, without vowels you would not know how it should be pronounced.

הוּא

But if you put a point in the middle of the *waw* ו, it becomes a vowel called a *shureq*, and the word will be pronounced HOO, which means "he."

הִיא

Then, if you replace the middle consonant by a *yod* י , and put a point under the *he* הִ, it becomes a vowel called a long *hireq*, and the pronoun is now pronounced HEE, but means "she," which is a little confusing for English-speaking people, to say the least.

הִוא

But there is yet another spelling of "she" in which the

middle consonant is a *waw* ו, rather than a *yod* י, and a point is placed under the *he* ה, called a short *hireq*. The pronoun is then pronounced HI, as in HIT.

    HOO   הוּא   "he"
           shureq

    HI(T)   הִוא   "she"
      short *hireq*

You can see how simple it would be for a copyist to put the Massoretic point in the wrong place. If he put it in the middle of the *waw* ו, it would mean "he"; or if he put it under the *he* ה, it would mean "she."

In the text itself the Hebrew verb "crush" is in the masculine form; but Lapide says it is quite common for a feminine subject to have masculine forms, when the action involved is considered manly, as is the case here:

> There are some Hebrew texts, which for הוּא read הִוא or הִיא, with a short or long *hireq*. Also הוּא *hu* is often used instead of הִיא *hi*, especially when there is some emphasis on action and something manly is predicated of the woman, as is the case here with the crushing of the serpent's head. Examples of this are found in this chapter in verses 12 and 20, also in Gen 17:14, 24:44, 28:21, and 28: 25. It makes no difference that the verb is masculine יָשׁוּף *yasuph*, that is "(he) shall crush," for it

The Third Meeting

often happens in Hebrew that the masculine is used instead of the feminine and vice versa, especially when there is an underlying reason or mystery, as I have just said. Therefore *hi yasuph* is used instead of *hi tasuph*. So in Genesis 2:13 it is said יקרא אשה *yickare isha,* ["*he* shall be called Woman"] instead of תקרא אשה *tickare isha,* ["*she* shall be called Woman"].[13]

Thus, Lapide is saying that there is nothing in the Hebrew grammar to prohibit a "she" reading, but that, on the contrary, the very Hebrew grammar reflects the underlying mystery involved. However, since the pre-Massoretic text most likely read simply הוא , just the consonants without the vowels, we have to go to Jewish tradition to find out whether the pronoun was pronounced HOO or HI, or even HEE.

Fr. Vawter mentioned that the Jewish philosopher Philo, who lived around 40 A.D., argued from the Hebrew poetic technique known as parellelism, that the reading should be "she." Genesis, since it is an historical book, is written in prose; but whenever a prophecy is uttered, as is the case here, Moses turns to poetry. In the technique of parallelism, the idea in one line parallels the idea in the following line; as, for instance, in Our Lady's Magnificat:

> My soul doth magnify the Lord.
>   And my spirit hath rejoiced in God my Savior
>   (Lk 1:46,47).

You can see that the ideas in the first line or *stich,* "soul"

The Woman of Genesis

and "Lord," complement the ideas "spirit" and "God" of the second line. In some cases, two lines, a *distich* or couplet, parallel a following couplet, as is the case in Genesis 3:15.

1	A	I shall put enmities between thee and the woman,
	B	and between thy seed and her seed:
2	A	She shall crush thy head,
	B	and thou shalt lie in wait for her heel.

In this case line 1A goes with line 2A, and line 1B corresponds to line 2B. Therefore the "woman" of line 1A corresponds with the "she" of line 2A. To make the subject of line 2A "he" or "it", and to say that it relates to the "seed" of line 1B, is bad Hebrew poetry according to Philo. Parallelism is, as it were, rhyming ideas, rather than rhyming sounds, and to read "he" in the context is a discordant idea. It would be as though an expected rhyming couplet in English did not rhyme, thus producing a discordant sound.

Lapide says another early Jewish witness is the historian Josephus, who died around 101 A.D.

> Whence also Josephus (Book I, Chap. 3) reads it this way, as our translator [Ruffinus] writes. For he says: "He ordained that the woman should inflict wounds on his head"...from which it is evident that Josephus in his day read *aute*, that is to say, "she."[14]

Josephus and Philo both wrote in Greek, but also knew Hebrew so their testimony is a common witness that the

The Third Meeting

Greek of the Septuagint of their day was *aute,* and that the Hebrew pronoun was pronounced HI or HEE.

Lapide also gives a much later witness, later even than the Massoretes, the Jewish philosopher, Moses Maimonides, who died about 1204. Of course, Maimonides did not believe in the Messianic or Mariological content of this prophecy, thinking that the woman of the context was merely Eve, but he obviously believed nevertheless that the text read "she."

> Moses Maimonides writes, which is indeed amazing, "But what must be admired most of all, is that the serpent is joined with Eve, that is, its seed with her seed, its head with her heel; that she (Eve) should conquer it (the serpent) in the head, and that it should conquer her in the heel." (*More Nebochim,* Part II, chap. 30).[15]

So, evidently, in Maimonides' day there were some Hebrew codices which read "she." Lapide says that a few of these ancient Hebrew codices have survived:

> Two Hebrew codices in the Vatican library have היא (according to Kennicott, numbers 227 and 239). Another from the Bernard de Rossi library has הוא . So also another so-called Onkelosi Codex [translation from the Hebrew into Aramaic] in the same library.[16]

Let us now examine the Greek translation of the Old Testament known as the Septuagint. The Septuagint,

The Woman of Genesis

which dates from around 250 B.C., has always had a very special place in the history of the Bible, and is never put on the same level as any other translation, such as the Douay-Rheims. The *New* Testament was inspired and written in Greek, but all its quotations from the *Old* Testament are from the Septuagint. Fr. Vawter mentioned that the version of the Septuagint which we now have reads *autos* "he," rather than *aute* "she," but gave no historical or critical analysis of the text.

Origen, an early Father of the Church, is probably the first textual critic, and one of the greatest. In 255 A.D. he completed his famous *Hexapla,* a Greek word meaning "six columns," in which he tried to recover the original text of the Septuagint. At the Jewish Council of Jamnia held in the year 100 A.D., it was decided to render a new Greek translation of the Hebrew Old Testament because there was concern about Christian apologists who were converting Jews by pointing out the Messianc prophecies in the Septuagint. These prophecies seem to come through more clearly in Greek even than in Hebrew.

Accordingly, three new Greek translations were eventually brought out by the Jewish scholars Aquila, Symmachus, and Theodotion. Thus, by Origen's time, there were four Greek versions in circulation. Origen arranged these versions in six columns: in the first column, the current Hebrew; in the second, the Hebrew text in Greek letters: in the third, the version of Aquila; in the fourth, that of Symmachus; in the fifth, the text of the Septuagint as it existed in his day; and finally, in the sixth column, that of Theodotion.

The Third Meeting

As if this wasn't complicated enough, three other anonymous translations of the Septuagint were discovered in Origen's day which became known as the *Quinta, Sexta,* and *Septima:* the Fifth, Sixth, and Seventh. Two of these versions were actually discovered by Origen himself, one of them in a jar near Jericho, seventeen centuries before the Dead Sea Scrolls were found near the very same area. The *Hexapla* remained in the library at Caesarea in Palestine, where it was consulted by St. Jerome when he was working on the Vulgate. Unfortunately, this great work was lost when the library was destroyed by fire during the sack of Caesarea by the Arabs in the year 653.

However, fragments of the *Hexapla* survived in the writings of the Fathers, and the great Benedictine biblical scholar, Bernard de Montfaucon, published a two-volume edition of these fragments in 1713. He gives the reading *autos,* "he," but adds: *Allos-aute* αλλος αυτή, "in another place—she":

> ...So some manuscripts; and this appears to have been the reading of some old translator, whose name we know not, and whom the translator of the Vulgate follows.[17]

Montfaucon is referring to the anonymous *Quinta, Sexta,* and *Septima,* which evidently read "she," and which St. Jerome could well have followed. But the majority of the Eastern Fathers who wrote in Greek read *autos,* "he," for our passage, with the exception of St. Ephraim who wrote in Syriac, and who reads "she." But, as I have noted earlier, this reading does not change the theological sense of the passage, and most of the Eastern Fathers understand the Woman of Genesis to be Our Lady. Let me read just one example. Here is St. Justin the Martyr, who died around 165 A.D., in his *Dialogue with Trypho the Jew:*

We understand that he [Christ] became man by means of the Virgin, so that the disobedience caused by the serpent might be destroyed just as it began. Eve, a virgin, having conceived the word of the serpent, gave birth to disobedience and death. Mary, on the other hand, conceiving faith and joy, when the Angel Gabriel announced to her that the Spirit of the Lord would come upon her and the power of the Most High would overshadow her so that the Holy One born of her would be called the Son of God, answered: "Be it done unto me according to thy word." He is then born of her, he of whom the Scriptures so often speak. By her, God destroyed the empire of the serpent and of all the angels and men who became like to the serpent, and frees from death those who repent of their faults and believe in him.[18]

Let me now proceed to the Latin Vulgate of St. Jerome, which reads *ipsa*, "she." We heard Fr. Vawter admit that at least from the time of St. Ambrose most of the Latin Fathers read *ipsa*, and that almost all the ancient manuscripts of the Vulgate which have survived render it "she." Now, the Latin Vulgate of St. Jerome is the only edition declared authentic by the Church, decreed so by the Council of Trent; and, since the Greek and Hebrew versions do not enjoy this distinction, the Vulgate possesses the greatest

The Third Meeting

authority. Let me read a few paragraphs from a wonderful old book by Richard Quigley, entitled *Ipse, Ipsa, Ipsum: Which? (He, She, It: Which?)*. It is the story of a controversy on the very topic under discussion here tonight: "He" versus "She," between the Anglican Bishop of Fredricton, New Brunswick, Dr. Kingden; his Vicar, Rev. Davenport; and Richard Quigley, a Catholic lawyer from St. John, New Brunswick:

> How are we to know what is the genuine Word of God? The Vicar can give no intelligible answer, because he has no conception of the character and office of the Church of God. The Catholic at once gives an answer in the words of St. Augustine: "I would not believe the Gospel were I not moved there to by the authority of the Catholic Church." So must it be with every man who looks the question fairly in the face. The Bible is the creation of the Church; and to accept it, in any true sense, as the Word of God, logically involves a belief in the infallibility of the Church. External authority is the only voucher for canonicity. It was for the Church here, as in doctrinal controversies, to judge of conflicting traditions and diverging opinions, and in the fullness of time to give her sentence. And in fact, she so judged, and judged infallibly, or her judgement is vain. The Vicar who hypocritically boasts of the "Bible-only" principle (thereby flatly contradicting his own school)[High-Church], prefers the opinion of the Quaker critic, Tregelles, to the authority of the Church of God. Well, that is consistent enough. In the first days of

The Woman of Genesis

Protestantism, private judgement fixed what the Scripture meant; now textual criticism settles for the Vicar what Scripture says: and shortly, "higher criticism" will reject text and meaning alike.[19]

The weakest argument in science is one from authority; so, since biblical criticism is admittedly a science, the liberal critics reject the argument from authority. But as I tried to point out at our last meeting, the Bible cannot be interpreted by biblical criticism alone, apart from the Tradition and the Magisterium of the Church. So let me turn then to the authority of Tradition and to the testimony of two of the great Doctors of the Church, St. Robert Bellarmine (d. 1621) and St. Alphonsus Maria Liguori (d. 1787). Here is St. Robert Bellarmine in his famous book *De Controversiis:*

> Such errors do not compromise the integrity required by Holy Scripture in matters of faith and morals. For the most part, the differences in the various readings lie in the divergence of languages, while little or nothing has changed in the meaning. But the errors which have resulted from the addition of the [Massoretic] points in no way compromise the truth, for they have been added from without, nor do they change the text. So we can remove the points and read otherwise.[20]

Therefore, St. Robert Bellarmine believes that the Hebrew version of the Bible we have today is substantially correct, but does contain some minor errors not pertaining to faith or morals which have been introduced mainly by a misreading of the Massoretic points. Now, the

The Third Meeting

Massoretic points are not inspired, and thus do not partake of the infallibility associated with the Bible and the Church. So nothing forbids us from changing the current points from הוּא to הִוא in order to make the reading conform to the *ipsa* "she" of the Latin Vulgate.

St. Alphonsus Maria Liguori is even more emphatic on this point. This is from his work, *The Divine Office:*

Actual Inferiority of the Hebrew Text

There is no doubt that the Hebrew text, being the original text, deserves, when considered by itself, to be preferred to all the versions; but the learned generally agree in saying that the original Hebrew is no longer perfectly exact. Indeed, Salmeron, Moririus, and others, teach that the Jews have altered it out of hatred for Christianity; many, with Bellarmine, think that many errors crept in through ignorance, or by the negligence of copyists. It should especially be remarked that, after the fifth century, the Jewish doctors called Massoretes have added to the Hebrew text signs never before seen, that is, points, which have taken the place of vowels, and that became the occasion of numerous equivocations and discordant interpretations.

Superiority and Authenticity of the Vulgate

The Council of Trent, therefore, did not wish to do for the Hebrew text what it did for the Latin text of the Vulgate: for the latter it declared authentic by presenting it as exempt from all error, at least in what concerns the dogmas of faith and moral precepts. Hence, in his dissertation on the transmission of the Holy Scriptures, Xavier Matthei concludes that, there being given no-matter-what Hebrew passage or text, and the Vulgate not agreeing with it, one should keep the Vulgate: "Not," he adds, "that this version is more authentic than the Hebrew text. but because it may be believed, on the one hand, that the passage in question is no longer to be found in the Hebrew as it was there primitively; on the other hand, that this primitive text is found exactly reproduced in the Vulgate—the only version that has merited to be approved by the Church."[21]

Therefore, St. Alphonsus Maria contends that when it comes down to a choice between the Hebrew and the Vulgate, as we have here, we should hold with the Vulgate. So I prefer the "she" reading of our text because of what I consider its greater authority, but also because of practical historical considerations. When the "she" reading was rejected by the Protestants in the sixteenth century, it was accompanied by a consequent decrease in devotion to the Blessed Virgin Mary. Now, Modernism is liberal Protestantism inside the Catholic Church, and the liberal Catholics who are currently trying to eliminate the "she" reading from our Catholic Bibles are admittedly engaged in a campaign to downgrade devotion to Our Blessed Lady. Let me conclude now by reading one more passage from Richard Quigley's *Ipse, Ipsa, Ipsum: Which?* His remarks about Protestants apply equally well to the liberal Catholics of our day.

The Third Meeting

The Anglo-Ritualist *Union Review* ... says: "It [Heresy regarding the Incarnation] prevails to a very great extent among English Churchmen, and its withering effects are very difficult to shake off even by those who have long since become orthodox in their theoretical creed." Terrible and affrighting confession! "It is also true," the *Review* adds, "and deserves consideration, that there has been hitherto no marked tendency to heresy on the subject of the Incarnation among Roman Catholics while, where the dignity of the Blessed Virgin has been undervalued, heresies have speedily crept in."[22]

In summary and conclusion, we see that we can make a good case for our "she" reading, especially from the Hebrew text and from Jewish tradition, but mainly from the authority of the Tradition and Magisterium of the Church. And although a "he" or "it" reading does not change the theological sense of our passage, such readings in the past have frequently been accompanied by a noticeable decline in devotion to Our Blessed Lady.

REFERENCES

1. Bruce Vawter, C.M., *A New Catholic Commentary on Holy Scripture*, the article *Genesis*, Thomas Nelson and Sons, London, 1969, p.181.
2. Vawter, *Op. cit.*, p.181.
3. *Idem*, p.181.
4. *Idem*, p.181.
5. *Idem*, p.181.
6. *Idem*, p.181.
7. *Idem*, p.181.
8. *Idem*, p.181.

9. *Idem*, p.181.
10. *Idem*, pp.181,182.
11. Cornelius a Lapide, *Commentaria in Scripturam Sacram*, Larousse, Paris, 1848, p.105.
12. Lapide, *Op. cit.*, p.106.
13. *Idem*, p.105
14. *Idem*, p.105
15. *Idem*, p.105
16. *Idem*, p.106
17. Richard Quigley, *Ipse, Ipsa, Ipsum: Which?* Fr. Pustet and Co., New York, 1890, p.338.
18. St. Justin Martyr, *Dialogue with Trypho the Jew*, (Chapter 100), quoted by Thomas C. Donlon, O.P., Francis L. B. Cunningham, O.P. and Augustine Rock, O.P. in *Christ and His Sacraments*, The Priory Press, Dubuque, IA, 1958, p.272.
19. Quigley, *Op. cit.*, pp.366,367.
20. St. Robert Bellarmine, *De Controversiis*, Book II, Chap. 2, Bellagate, Milan, 1721, p.74.
21. St. Alphonsus Maria Liguori, *The Divine Office*, Benziger Brothers, New York, 1890, pp.19,20.
22. *Idem, p.224.*

THE FOURTH MEETING

"Bruise" versus "Crush"

Fr. Robert A. Staatz

Good evening, and welcome to the conclusion of our dialogue. Tonight let me commence right where we left off, with the article on Genesis by Bruce Vawter in a *New Catholic Commentary on Holy Scripture:*

"It will crush your head, and you will crush its heel" [If you remember, Fr. Vawter preferred "it" to the "he" of the Revised Standard, because the pronoun refers to "seed," a neuter collective noun]: alternately, "It will watch for your head, and you will watch for its heel." What is certain is that the same verb *shuph* is used in each case, and hence the translation should be the same. What is not certain is the translation. The verb appears elsewhere only in Jb 9:17 "he crushes me with a tempest" (Revised Standard Version)...The Septuagint translated as though the verb were *shur* "watch for." The *Vetus Latinus* [The *Old Latin* version which preceded the Vulgate of Jerome] reproduced the Septuagint: "He will watch for your head, and you will watch for his heel." Jerome compromised, as he often did, with popular opinion, translating the verb in the first instance *conteret* ["bruise" or "crush"] with the Hebrew, and in the second *insidiaberis* ["lie in wait for"]

The Woman of Genesis

with the Septuagint. However in his *Liber Hebraicarum Quaestionum in Genesim [The Book of Hebrew Questions in Genesis]* he observes, having noted the *Vetus Latinus:* "The Hebrew has it better, 'He will bruise your head, and you will bruise his heel'; because the serpent lies in wait even for our footsteps: and the Lord will speedily crush Satan under our feet" (PL 28, 1981). Whatever the precise meaning of the Hebrew verb, we have in this passage an announcement of the continuous struggle that must exist between mankind and the evil that will try to dominate man, a struggle in which God is very much concerned.[1]

The Douay-Rheims has two different verbs in the second couplet, namely "crush" and "lie in wait for." But only one verb is used in the Hebrew, namely *shuph*, which can mean "bruise" or "crush." So the Revised Standard, which follows the Hebrew, reads:

> He will bruise your head
> and you will bruise his heel.

Now, the Greek Septuagint also has only one verb *tereo* which is where we get our name Teresa, and which means "watch for" or "lie in wait for." So the Septuagint reads:

> He will watch for your head
> and you will watch for his heel.

What Jerome did, then, was to compromise between the Hebrew and the Greek, by taking the first verb from the Hebrew and the second from the Greek:

The Fourth Meeting

> (She) shall *crush* your head
> and you shall *lie in wait for* (her) heel.

Jerome's scholarship, unfortunately, was greatly hampered by the limited resources available in his day. Here is a typical recent comment on Jerome's scholarship by the Jesuit John McKenzie, from his article on Job in his excellent *Dictionary of the Bible:*

> The Vulgate translation of [Job] 19:25, 26, which introduces the idea of the resurrection into Job, is an unfaithful translation of a corrupted Hebrew text. The idea can be traced nowhere else in the speeches of Job; and it is so relevant to the problem that it is most unlikely that it would be mentioned only once and then dismissed. Nevertheless, Job wonders whether there may not be some possibility of a future vindication which ordinary experience does not offer. It is possible that the author leads the discussion towards this point but does not carry it further. Hebrew belief of the period presented nothing to which he could carry it.[2]

The passage McKenzie is referring to in the older Douay-Rheims, which follows the Vulgate closely, reads:

> For I know that my Redeemer liveth,
> and in the last day I shall rise out of the earth.
> And I shall be clothed again with my skin,
> and in my flesh I shall see my God.

It is uncertain at what time the book of Job was written;

opinions vary from the time of the patriarchs to the time of the prophets. But since the book is full of Hebrew archaisms, it seems safe to assign it a fairly early date. What is certain is that, at such an early date, the book could not possibly have treated so explicity of the resurrection of the body. That doctrine was a late development in the religious history of the Jews, probably dating from the time of the Machabees. Today, biblical scholars have a much better knowledge of Hebrew than that which was available to Jerome, and better texts from which to work. Also, they are much more careful in our day not to read things piously into the Bible which are really not there. Let me go back now to Bruce Vawter's article on Genesis:

> Do we also have an announcement of the eventual victory that mankind will win? Everyone will agree that the text contains "less a promise of victory than of perpetual strife" (McKenzie, *The Two-Edged Sword*, p.104). However, probably most commentators will also find a prediction of victory implied in the figure that is employed (a human foot crushing the head of the serpent whose fangs, in turn, are imbedded in its heel) and in the fact that this is a struggle willed by God, the outcome of which, in view of *Heilsgeschichte* ["salvation history"], can only be victory...Thus we have a basis for finding the *Reparatoris futuri promissio* ["promise of a future Redeemer"] of which the Biblical Commission spoke in 1909...The soteriology of this passage, however, was not to be fully grasped until the New Testament had revealed the manner in which man's victory over the serpent was attained;

The Fourth Meeting

and even then the Fathers are by no means in agreement as to how the text was to be fitted into the Messianic history.[3]

Since the Hebrew verb *shuph* can mean either "bruise" or "crush," why do most modern biblical scholars prefer the "bruise" of the Revised Standard Version to the "crush" of the Douay-Rheims? It is because the word "bruise" gives a better impression of an on-going struggle, rather than the complete Messianic victory of the word "crush." Let us look at the complete quote referred to by Vawter from McKenzie's *Two-Edged Sword:*

> Theological interest in recent years has centered even more on that verse of this passage which is called "the beginning of the Gospel" *[Protoevangelium]:* "I will place enmity between you (the serpent) and the woman, between your seed and her seed; it shall wound (?) your head, and you shall wound (?) its heel." The figure of the serpent strikes at his foot. In the context, the line is less a promise of victory than of perpetual strife; but it is a strife, at least, in which the man is not foredoomed to defeat. We are not even certain of the meaning of the key word *[shuph].* But the line is not always read in context. Did the Hebrew storyteller see in the vision the figure of the Man who was to overcome sin and death on behalf of the race? We must measure the clarity of his vision by the clarity of his enunciation, because we have no other measure; and the enunciation is most obscure. Still less can we detect in his mind any awareness of the mother of Jesus; she who was to be truly the Ideal

The Woman of Genesis

Woman, and who was to raise her sex to a dignity undreamed, was too great a figure for the comprehension of those times.[4]

Now, Mrs. Stepan's favorite argument is the one from authority, the authority of the Tradition and Magisterium of the Church; and she accuses liberals, like myself, of rejecting this argument. On the contrary, I have saved my argument from authority till the very end. Rome has recently issued a new version of the Latin Vulgate of Jerome called the Neo-Vulgate. This new Latin version which was done with the assistance of Protestant and Jewish scholars, incorporates all the recent discoveries of biblical criticism into its text. Here, then, is the new Latin version of Genesis 3:15

> *Inimicitias ponam inter te et mulierem*
> *et semen tuum et semen illius;*
> *Ipsum conteret caput tuum,*
> *et tu conteres calcaneum eius.*[5]

This translates:

> I will put enmity between you and the woman,
>   and your seed and that one's seed;
> It shall bruise your head,
>   and you shall bruise its heel.

This is, of course, basically the same as the old King James Version:

> I will put enmity between thee and the woman,

The Fourth Meeting

and thy seed and her seed:
It shall bruise thy head
and thou shall bruise his heel.

Bruce Vawter said, if you remember, that "it" would be more proper than the "he" of the Revised Standard, since the pronoun refers to the neuter collective noun "seed." The Neo-Vulgate is designed to be the typical text of the Latin Church, which means that it will appear in all official documents coming from the Vatican. It is also intended to be used as a norm for Catholic translations into all vernacular languages, including English.

Mrs. Maria Stepan

After what we have just heard about the scholarship of St. Jerome, I first feel compelled to say something in his praise. Let me just read the opening paragraph from Pope Benedict XV's encyclical *Spiritus Paraclitus* which appeared in 1920, the fifteenth centenary of the death of this holy and eminent Doctor of the Church:

> Since the Holy Spirit, the Comforter, had bestowed the Sciptures on the human race for their instruction in Divine things, He also raised up in successive ages saintly and learned men whose task it should be to develop that treasure and so provide for the faithful plenteous "consolation from the Scriptures" (Rom 15:4). Foremost among these teachers stands St. Jerome. Him the Catholic Church acclaims and reveres as her "Greatest Doctor," divinely given her for the understanding of the Bible.[6]

The Woman of Genesis

We have seen that the liberal Catholic biblical scholars seem to be quite a bit behind-the-times with regard to the impact of archaeology on biblical studies. The recent discoveries at Ebla support both the Mosaic authenticity of the Pentateuch and refute the claims of the *Religionsgeschichte* concerning the history and evolution of doctrine. Likewise, the discovery at Ras Shamra in Syria of the ancient city of Ugarit refutes the claim of the liberals, that the doctrine of the resurrection could not have been stated in the book of Job since that doctrine did not develop until the post-exilic period.

Now, most of the Psalms traditionally were believed to have been written by David who lived around 1000 B.C., but again because of their highly developed doctrine they were assigned by the liberals to the post-exilic period, that is after 400 B.C. The royal archives of Ugarit were discovered in 1930, and these texts have had an immense impact on Psalms scholarship. The ancient city of Ugarit was destroyed in 1200 B.C., so this dates the Ugaritic texts well before the time of David. Let me read a few comments on the significance of these texts by Edwin Yamauchi in his outstanding introduction to biblical archaeology, *The Stones and the Scriptures:*

> Critical scholars following the lead of Wellhausen and Duhm dated the Psalms to the post-Exilic period because their level of religion seemed too advanced for an earlier age. R.H. Pfeiffer dated the great majority of the Psalms between 400 and 100 B.C. in his introduction to the Old Testament published in 1941. The discoveries at Ugarit...have shown that the Psalms are to be dated early rather than late in Israel's history. Many scholars have shown that the Ugaritic texts

The Fourth Meeting

yield exact parallels to the poetic patterns and verbal combinations of the Psalms, Proverbs, and other biblical texts. As Ugarit was destroyed c. 1200 B.C., these parallels imply an early date. Albright comments: "Actually much early Hebrew verse dates from the second millenium, and was composed in a poetic dialect closely related to the generalized epic dialect of Canaan in which Ugaritic verse was composed."[7]

The great Catholic authority on the Ugaritic texts is Fr. Mitchell Dahood, S.J., who has recently produced a new translation of the Psalms, aided by the insights he has acquired by his studies of these texts. Fr. Dahood argues that most of the Psalms should indeed be assigned to the time of David as was traditionally believed, and that they reveal a clear belief in such doctrines as the final judgment, the resurrection, and the beatific vision. Fr. Dahood builds up his case verse by verse, and word by word, until the final cumulative effect is overwhelming. Let me give just one example from a multitude of his technique. This is his translation of Psalm 7 (16):15:

> At the vindication
>   I will gaze upon your face;
> At the resurrection
>   I will be saturated with your being.

At the vindication. In other words, at the final judgment when I shall be vindicated. The parallel with "at the resurrection" proves that the psalmist is dealing with the final judgment, as in Ps 1:5...
At the resurrection. This seems to be plain sense of

behakis when one compares it with the eschatological passages in Isa 26:19, "But your dead will live, their bodies will rise. Arise *(hakisu)* and sing. O you who dwell in the slime," and Dan 12:2, "And many of those who sleep in the land of the slime will arise *(yakisu),* some to everlasting life, and others to everlasting reproach and contempt."

your being. Temunah describes the "form" or "figure" of God as he appeared to Moses. Num 12:8 states that Moses alone was permitted to behold the *temunah* of Yahweh, but the psalmist is confident that he will receive this privilege after the final judgment . . .

> In the Ugaritic textbooks 68:17-18, one reads *Itugsu puth lydlp tmnh* . . . The existence of *tmn* [the consonants of *temunah]* in Ugaritic bespeaks the antiquity of the substantive; its occurrence in Ps 17 comports well with the archaic language throughout the psalm that the Israelite belief in the beatific vision was very ancient indeed.[8]

From the archaic language used throughout, Fr. Dahood concludes that this Psalm should be dated early rather than late, and indeed could well have been written by David himself as its superscription, "A Prayer of David," suggests. This would date belief in the final judgment, the resurrection, and the beatific vision, to at least 1000 B.C., or earlier than any liberal scholar would date the book of Job. It is therefore thoroughly unscholarly to deny the possibility of belief in the resurrection of the body in the book of Job, and is purely the result of an unscientific *religionsgeschichtliches* bias.

The Fourth Meeting

As I mentioned previously, Protestant fundamentalists like to use the phrase "archaeology proves the Bible." But again I am equally fascinated by the fact that archaeology always supports the Magisterium. So I can't resist mentioning that in 1910 a decision of the Biblical Commission condemned the still-current liberal opinion assigning the bulk of the Psalms to the post-Exilic period because of their highly developed doctrinal content.

Let me go on now to Fr. Staatz's remarks about the Neo-Vulgate which is intended, he says, to replace the Vulgate of St. Jerome. This Neo-Vulgate edition has been made for the most part from the Massoretic Hebrew text, which most scholars will admit has been corrupted in many critical passages. The Hebrew codices date only as far back as the early Middle Ages; and with the discovery of the Dead Sea Scrolls, some of which date from around 100 B.C., it will be possible in a few years, one would hope, to bring out a much more critical edition of the Hebrew Bible. A case in point is the book of Isaiah which was found completely intact at Qumran and is dated around 100 B.C. Predictably, this Isaiah text is much closer to the Septuagint than the Massoretic text of today. The Septuagint has always been in Christian hands, but after the destruction of Jerusalem, when the small Jewish-Christian community was absorbed into the main body of the Gentile Church, a tradition of Hebrew scholarship died out in the early Church until it was revived by St. Jerome.

Over the course of the years, a few copyist errors had crept into the Vulgate of St. Jerome, and the Neo-Vulgate was supposed to recover the original text. Many traditional Catholic biblical scholars have complained to Rome that this new text, far from being a revision of the Vulgate as was intended, is rather a new interpretation—an interpretation aimed at bringing the Bible into line with the so-called "recent discoveries" of biblical criticism, which in many cases, as we have seen, contradict the authentic Tradition and Magisterium of the Church. There is, however, no question of the infallibility of the Church involved here, because the rescript issuing the Neo-Vulgate contained no "in perpetuities" or anathemas, etc., as was the case with the Sixto-Clementine Vulgate which preceded it. Many traditional scholars feel that the Neo-Vulgate will soon be found wanting and gradually dropped, as happened with a new Latin translation of the Psalms issued by Cardinal Bea a few years ago.

I come now to the topic at hand—"crush" versus "bruise"—and I will follow the same procedure I did the last time, namely, to go through the Hebrew, Greek, and Latin versions of our text in that order. As you recall, Fr. Vawter claimed that, with regard to the Hebrew text, "the same verb *shuph* is used in each case, and hence the translation should be the same," namely "bruise." But this is not necessarily true. The same word can have quite different meanings in any language, including Hebrew. Now, I have just opened a dictionary at random, and find:

summary (adj.) 1. comprehensive—as in "a summary account";
                2. without delay—as in "summary vengeance."

Therefore, let us look up the Hebrew word *shuph* in a recognized Hebrew lexicon (Koehler-Baumgartner, 1967 edition):

The Fourth Meeting

שׁוּף *shuph,* (verb) 1. A by-form of שָׁאַף *sha'aph* (see Brown, Driver, and Briggs); "to trample upon, crush"; Akkadian cognate *shapu,* "to trample underfoot"; Syriac, "to rub, wear out, bruise."

שׁוּף *shuph,* (verb) 2. Arabic cognate *shapa,* "to see, look at, watch."

Thus, we see that there are two distinct meanings for the verb *shuph;* and also that *shuph* 1. is derived, according to Brown, Driver and Briggs, the authors of another Hebrew lexicon, from the older verb *sha'aph,* which means "to trample upon." This means we are dealing here with two distinct but similar Hebrew roots, a situation employed in a Hebrew poetic technique known as *paranomasia,* or word play. Word play is also used in English poetry, or in any language where words have several layers of meaning. So a Hebrew would be aware of a double-meaning play on words as he read our passage: the woman is lying in wait to crush the serpent, while the serpent is waiting to be crushed. Now, the amazing thing about this particular *paranomasia* is that it also comes across even in Greek, where the word for "crush" is *teiro,* and the word for "lie in wait for" is *tereo,* which are so similar. This gives us some idea why St. Augustine considered the Septuagint at least protectively inspired. Unfortunately, this word play does not come through in Latin, where the word for "crush" is *conteret* and the word for "lie in wait for" is *insidiaberis;* nor, of course, does it transpose into English. Let me elaborate on the Greek.

(Mrs. Stepan writes on the blackboard as she speaks.)

The Woman of Genesis

teiresei τειρήσει, "will crush"
 epsilon ε, *iota* ι
tereseis τηρήσεις "will lie in wait for"
 eta η

The edition of the Septuagint which I have in hand is published by Samuel Bagster and Sons of London. The text itself reads *teresei* τηρήσει, "will lie in wait for," and *tereseis* τηρήσεις, "you will lie in wait for." Then, in a footnote we find the variant reading *teiresei* τειρήσει, "will crush," and *teireseis* τειρήσεις, "you will crush." You can see how close *teiresei* and *tereseis* are, and how easy it would have been for a copyist to have made a mistake —it was getting late, he was tired, the lamp was flickering, etc.; and he accidentally repeated the *epsilon* ε and the *iota* ι instead of writing the intended *eta* η.

And now to the Latin of St. Jerome. I can picture St. Jerome with the Hebrew text before him, wondering how to translate the two verbs *yashuphka...tashuphnu*. He could also have had two alternate readings of the Septuagint before him, one of which read *teresei...tereseis*, and the other *teiresei...teireseis*. Now I am sure St. Jerome knew that the verb *shuph* could mean either "crush" or "lie in wait for," so I can imagine him arranging the verbs into a diagram to contrast the various possibilities in order to see which combination made the most sense:

1) She will lie in wait for...you will lie in wait for
2) She will crush...you will crush
3) She will lie in wait for...you will crush

78

The Fourth Meeting

4) She will crush...you will lie in wait for

1) *She will lie in wait for...you will lie in wait for.* This was Fr. Vawter's suggested translation of the Septuagint. "He will watch for your head, and you will watch for his heel." This makes no sense in the context of a curse upon the serpent. There is no victory, not even a struggle; the serpent and the woman simply watch one another interminably.

2) *She will crush...you will crush.* This is the same as the Revised Standard Version, "He will bruise your head and you will bruise his heel." There is no victory here, only a struggle, which seems almost to end in a draw. Again, this makes little sense in the context of a curse upon the serpent, an announcement of a continuous war between the serpent and the promise of a future total victory for the woman. To promise the serpent even a partial victory in the context seems inappropriate.

3) *She will lie in wait for...you will crush.* Of course, this is absolutely untenable; the victory would go to the serpent.

4) *She will crush...you will lie in wait for.* I am sure that St. Jerome decided this was the only possibility that made any sense in the given context, even though he couldn't catch in Latin the word-play of the Hebrew and the Greek, since the word in Latin for "crush" is *conteret* and for "lie in wait for" is *insidiaberis*. But what comes through is St. Jerome's powerful image of the crushing foot of the woman and the serpent's terror-stricken view of her heel. "The devils also believe and tremble" (Jas 2:19).

That St. Jerome went through some kind of a trial and error process such as this seems also to be the opinion of Cornelius a Lapide:

The Woman of Genesis

The word *shuph* which occurs twice in this declaration, has been rendered in many ways by interpreters. One can, however, quickly reduce them all to the two most important: one is *conterere*, "to crush" or "trample under foot,"...and the other *latenter observare*, "to watching from hiding," or *insidias struere*, "to set up snares." The translator of the Vulgate, as though undecided between the two, first took the word in one of these meanings, then the other. However, this translation is by far the most suitable for the whole passage.[9]

So much for the Bible itself; let me now appeal to the Magisterium of the Church. In 1854 Pope Pius IX issued his famous bull *Ineffabilis Deus*, defining the Immaculate Conception of Our Lady, which reads in part:

> Hence, just as Christ, the Mediator between God and man, assuming human nature, blotted out the handwriting of the decree that stood against us, and fastened it triumphantly to the Cross, so the Most Holy Virgin, united with Him by a most intimate and indissoluble bond, was, with Him and through Him, eternally at enmity with the evil Serpent, and most completely triumphed over him, and thus crushed his head with her immaculate foot.[10]

And here is Pope Pius XII's definition of the Assumption of Our Lady in 1950, in the bull *Munificentissimus Deus*:

The Fourth Meeting

Mary as the New Eve

We must remember especially that, since the second century, the Virgin Mary has been designated by the Holy Fathers as the new Eve, who, although subject to the new Adam, is most intimately associated with Him in that struggle against the infernal foe which, as foretold in the *Protoevangelium*, would finally result in that most complete victory over sin and death which are always associated in the writings of the Apostle of the Gentiles.[11]

If you remember, both Fr. Vawter and Fr. McKenzie contend that Genesis contained no clear reference to Our Lady, and Fr. Vawter added that Revelation 12 also had no reference to her. Revelation 12 is the chapter in which "a woman clothed with the sun" fights against a "great red Dragon." Here is an excerpt from Pope Paul VI's marvelous encyclical *Marialis Cultus:*

> The Bible is replete with the mystery of the Savior, and from Genesis to the Book of Revelation also contains clear references to her who was the Mother and associate of the Savior.[12]

Let me conclude with an account of two private revelations which have been approved by the Church, and which we should not overlook: the apparition of Our Lady to Juan Diego in Mexico in 1531, and her apparition to St.

The Woman of Genesis

Catherine Laboure in Paris in 1830. In the beautiful miraculous picture of Our Lady of Guadalupe, Mary is surrounded by the rays of the sun, so she is the "woman clothed with the sun" of Revelation 12. Here is how she became known as Our Lady of Guadalupe:

> Neither Bishop Zumarraga nor any other Spanish prelate has been able to explain why she wished to be called *de Guadalupe*. The reason must be that she did not say the phrase at all. She spoke in the Indian language and the combination of words which she used must have sounded like *de Guadalupe* to the Spaniards. The Aztec *te coatlaxopeuh* has a similar sound (it is pronounced *te quatlasupe*).
>
> *Te*, means "stone"; *coa* means "serpent"; *tha* is the noun ending which can be interpreted as "the"; while *xopeuh* means "crush" or "stamp out." The last part of the message has to be rearranged in the following manner in order to reveal its true meaning:
>
> "Her precious image will thus be known (by the name of) the Entirely Perfect Virgin, Holy Mary, and it will crush, stamp out, abolish, or eradicate the stone serpent."
>
> Mary's words here have more than one meaning. The "stone serpent" she refers to is clearly the feathered serpent-god of the Aztecs, Quetzalcoatl. Quetzalcoatl was one of several Aztec gods to whom the Indians annually offered over 20,000 men, women, and children in bloody sacrifice. However, by calling herself the Entirely Perfect Virgin, Mary indicates that the stone serpent was more than just a local problem—horrible as that problem was.

The Fourth Meeting

Precisely as the Entirely Perfect or Immaculate Virgin, Mary has always been identified by the Church with the Woman prophesied in Genesis: "The Lord said to the serpent...I will establish a feud between thee and the woman, between thy offspring and hers; she is to crush thy head, while thou dost lie in ambush at her heels." (Knox translation).... The Apocalypse identifies the serpent as Satan: "He made prisoner of the dragon, serpent of the primal age, whom we call the devil, or Satan" (20:2).

Mary's words then indicate that the stone serpent is really Satan. Subsequently, she actually destroyed the tyrannical domination of the stone serpent—Satan—by bringing about the astounding conversion of eight million Indians in the next seven years. Nothing like this has ever happened in the history of Christianity and it indicates that the Woman, the Entirely Perfect Virgin, has begun the final stages of her God-inspired struggle with the ancient serpent.[13]

And finally, in the apparition to St. Catherine Laboure, Our Lady herself indicated by a series of visions the design of the beautiful medal now known as the "Miraculous Medal":

> On the 27th of November 1830, at half past five in the evening, the hour of meditation for the community, the Blessed Virgin again showed herself to Sister Catherine as she knelt in the chapel among her companions.
>
> The Virgin, elevated about ten feet, appeared on the right side exactly where at present is the altar of "The Virgin of the Globe"....

The Woman of Genesis

Standing on the terrestrial sphere, her foot crushing the infernal serpent, Mary held in her hands, which were raised slightly above her waist, a smaller globe which she seemed to offer to God in a gesture of supplication.[14]

Thus it appears that both the Church and Our Lady herself are aware that it is she who is destined to crush completely the head of the serpent. Let us pray that she does so quickly.

REFERENCES

1. Bruce Vawter, C.M., in the article *Genesis* in *A New Catholic Commentary on Holy Scripture*, Thomas Nelson and Sons, London, 1969, p.181.
2. John Mckenzie, S.J., *Dictionary of the Bible*, Bruce Publishing Co., Milwaukee, 1965, p.441.
3. Vawter, *Op. cit.*, p.181.
4. John Mckenzie, S.J., *The Two-Edged Sword*, Bruce Publishing Co., Milwaukee, 1956, p.104.
5. *Nova Vulgata Bibliorum*, Libreria Editrice Vaticana, 1977, p.14.
6. Benedict XV, *Spiritus Paraclitus*, 1920; reprinted in *Rome and the Study of Scripture*, Abbey Press, St. Meinrad, IN, 1964, p.43.
7. Edwin Yamauchi, *The Stones and the Scriptures*, J.B. Lippincott Company, Philadelphia, 1972, pp.65,66.
8. Mitchell Dahood, S.J., *Psalms I*, The Anchor Bible, Doubleday and Co., Garden City, NY, 1965, pp.99,100
9. Cornelius a Lapide, *Commentaria in Scripturam Sacram*, Larousse, Paris, 1848, p.106.
10. Pius IX, *Ineffabilis Deus*, 1854; reprinted in *Papal Teachings: Our Lady*, Benedictines of Solesmes, St. Paul Editions, Boston, 1961, p.72.
11. Pius XII, *Munificentissimus Deus*, 1950; reprinted in *Papal Teachings: Our Lady*, p.317.
12. Paul VI, *Marialis Cultus*, 1974; Daughters of St. Paul, Boston, 1974, p.28.
13. Dr. Charles Wahlig and Fr. Bernard Geiger, O.F.M., Conv., *What is Guadalupe?* reprinted in *A Handbook on Guadalupe*, Prow Books, Franciscan Marytown Press, Libertyville, IL, 1974, pp.18-20.
14. *Saint Catherine Laboure*, M. Lescuyer et Fils, Paris, 1947, p.23

WORKS CITED

Bellarmine, St. Robert, *De Controversiis*,
Bellagate, Milan, 1721.

Benedict XV, Pope, *Spiritus Paraclitus*,
Rome and the Study of Scripture,
Abbey Press, St. Meinrad, IN, 1964.

Dahood, Mitchell, S.J., *Psalms I, The Anchor Bible*,
Doubleday and Co., Garden City, NY, 1965.

Ellis, Peter, C.SS.R., *The Men and the Message of the Old Testament*,
Liturgical Press, Collegeville, MN, 1963.

Garrigan, Fr. Owen, *Man's Intervention in Nature*,
Hawthorne Books, New York, 1967.

Jesuit Fathers of St. Mary's College, *The Church Teaches*,
B. Herder Book Co., St. Louis, 1955.

Justin Martyr, St., *Dialogue with Trypho the Jew*,
Donlon, Thomas C., O.P., Cunningham, Francis L. B., O.P., and Rock, Augustine, O.P., *Christ and His Sacraments*,
The Priory Press, Dubuque, IA, 1958.

Works Cited

Kevane, Msgr. Eugene, *Creed and Catechetics*,
  Christian Classics, Westminster, MD, 1978.

Lapide, Cornelius a, *Commentaria in Scripturam Sacram*,
  Larousse, Paris, 1848.

Liguori, St. Alphonsus Maria, *The Divine Office*,
  Benziger Brothers, New York, 1890.

McKenzie, John, S.J., *Dictionary of the Bible*,
  Bruce Publishing Co., Milwaukee, 1965.

Nova Vulgata Bibliorum,
  Libreria Editrice Vaticana, 1977.

O'Connell, Fr. Patrick, *Original Sin in the Light of Present-Day Science*,
  Lumen Christi Press, Houston, 1973.

Paul VI, Pope, *Marialis Cultus*,
  Daughters of St. Paul, Boston, 1974.

Pius IX, Pope, *Ineffabilis Deus*,
Doheny, Msgr. William and Kelly, Fr. Joseph,
Papal Documents on Mary,
  Bruce Publishing Co., Milwaukee, 1954.

Pius XII, Pope, *Divino Afflante Spiritu*,
Rome and the Study of Scripture,
  Abbey Press, St. Meinrad, IN, 1964.

The Woman of Genesis

Pius XII, Pope, *Humani Generis*,
  Weston College Press, Weston, MA, 1951.

Pius XII, Pope, *Munificentissimus Deus*,
Doheny, Msgr. William and Kelly, Fr. Joseph, *Papal Documents on Mary*,
  Bruce Publishing Co., Milwaukee, 1954.

Quigley, Richard, *Ipse, Ipsa, Ipsum: Which?*
  Frederick Pustet, New York, 1890.

Rome and the Study of Scripture,
  Abbey Press, St. Meinrad, IN, 1964.

Saint Catherine Laboure,
  M. Lescuyer et Fils, Paris, 1947.

Schumacher, Msgr. Leo, *The Truth about Teilhard*,
  Twin Circle Publishing Co., New York, 1968.

Steinmueller, Msgr. John, *A Companion to Scripture Studies*, Vol. 2,
  Lumen Christi Press, Houston, 1969.

Steinmueller, Msgr. John and Sullivan, Sr. Katherine, R.S.C.J., *Catholic Biblical Encyclopedia*,
  Joseph F. Wagner, New York, 1950.

Taguchi, Cardinal Paul, *The Study of Scripture*,
  L'Osservatore Romano, May 15, 1975, Vatican City.

Works Cited

Vawter, Bruce, C.M., *Genesis*,
Fuller, Johnston and Kearns, *A New Catholic Commentary*,
   Thomas Nelson and Sons, London, 1969.

Wahlig, Dr. Charles and Geiger, Bernard, O.F.M. Conv., *What is Guadalupe? A Handbook on Guadalupe*,
   Prow Books, Franciscan Marytown Press, Libertyville, IL, 1974.

Wilson, Clifford, *Ebla Tablets: Secrets of a Forgotten City*,
   Master Books, Creaton-Life Publishers, San Diego, CA, 1979.

Yamauchi, Edwin, *The Stones and the Scriptures*,
   J. B. Lippincott Co., Philadelphia, 1972.

Prayer of St. Maximilian Mary Kolbe

O Immaculate Queen of heaven and earth, refuge of sinners and our most loving Mother, whom God has made the treasurer of His mercy, I, an unworthy sinner, throw myself at your most holy feet and humbly beseech you to accept me, whole and entire, as your property.

To you, O Mother, I offer all the faculties of my soul and body, and I place my life, my death, my eternity in your hands, that you may use my entire being according to your will. Use me, O Immaculate Virgin, as you will to fulfill that which was written of you—"She shall crush your head," and "You have destroyed all heresies throughout the world."

Deign that I may become in your most pure and merciful hands a useful instrument to make you known and loved by so many erring and indifferent souls, and also to increase as much as possible the number of those who truly admire and love you, in order that the Kingdom of the Most Sacred Heart of Jesus may be spread throughout the world.

This I can do, O Most Holy Mother Immaculate, only with your help, for wherever you bestow your grace, there alone can the conversion and sanctification of souls be achieved, and there alone can the Kingdom of the Most Sacred Heart of Jesus be established.

A List of Other Small Books Available from Loreto Publications

Counsels to Confessors - Saint Leonard of Port Maurice	$6.95
Treatise on the Spiritual Life - Saint Vincent Ferrer	$5.96
The Storm Novena - Saint Benedict the Moor Mission	$4.95
The Dogma of Faith - Saint Benedict Center	$4.95
Boy Heroes - Dom Alban Fruth O.S.B.	$4.95
Breaking With the Past - Francis Aidan Gasquet, O.S.B.	$5.95
50 Meditations on the Passion - Alban Goodier, S.J.	$5.95
The Wisdom of Saint Francis DeSales	$5.95
Meet Brother Martin (dePorres) - Norbert Georges, O.P.	$5.95
Explanation of the Veni Sancte Spiritus - Fr. Nicholas Gihr	$6.95
Our Lady of Perpetual Help - Francis J. O' Connell, C.SS.R.	$5.95
The Poetry of Joseph Mary Plunkett	$6.95
The Conversion of Marie-Alphonse Ratisbonne	$6.95
The Wife Desired - Fr. Leo Kinsella	$7.95
The Man for Her - Fr. Leo Kinsella	$7.95
The Poems of Virginia Teehan	$6.95

Loreto Publications
P. O. Box 603
Fitzwilliam, NH 03447
Phone: 603-239-6671
www.LoretoPubs.org

THE GREAT COMMENTARY on THE FOUR GOSPELS by Cornelius aLapide, S.J.

QUOTES FROM THE REVIEW by SCOTT HAHN

Cornelius aLapide, S.J. (1568-1637) is a giant figure in the history of Catholic biblical interpretation. Born in a tiny Catholic enclave in the Calvinist Netherlands in the bloody generation after the Reformation, Lapide grew to be one of the Church's most gifted scholars and spiritual interpreters of the sacred page.

Between 1614 and 1645, Lapide wrote commentaries on every book of Scripture except Job and Psalms.

To read Lapide four hundred years later is to enter a nearly forgotten world of biblical interpretation ...more striking – the sheer breadth and density of Lapide's interpretative matrix or his audacity in summoning all these resources to the interpretation of the sacred text.

Lapide himself takes a breathtaking high view of Scripture's purpose: Lapide prefaces his commentary with thirty-eight "canons of interpretation," which reflect a wise and prayerful method. "

It is clear that the Fathers hold pride of place for Lapide in his interpretative work.

- *6"x 9" Book format*
- *2900+ Pages in four volumes*
- *First complete English translation*
- *Sewn Binding & Headbands*
- *Bonded Leather Covers & Satin Ribbons*
- *Greatest Catholic Bible Commentary ever*
- *Extensive discussion of Greek and Hebrew words*
- *$199. Per four volume set*